An Introduction to MATLAB for Behavioral Researchers

CHRISTOPHER R. MADAN

BIRMINGHAM CITY UNIVERSITY LIBRARY

$SAGE

Los Angeles | London | New Delhi
Singapore | Washington DC

Los Angeles | London | New Delhi
Singapore | Washington DC

FOR INFORMATION:

SAGE Publications, Inc.

2455 Teller Road

Thousand Oaks, California 91320

E-mail: order@sagepub.com

SAGE Publications Ltd.

1 Oliver's Yard

55 City Road

London EC1Y 1SP

United Kingdom

SAGE Publications India Pvt. Ltd.

B 1/I 1 Mohan Cooperative Industrial Area

Mathura Road, New Delhi 110 044

India

SAGE Publications Asia-Pacific Pte. Ltd.

3 Church Street

#10-04 Samsung Hub

Singapore 049483

Acquisitions Editor: Helen Salmon

Editorial Assistant: Kaitlin Coghill

Assistant Editor: Katie Guarino

Production Editor: Libby Larson

Copy Editor: QuADS

Typesetter: C&M Digitals (P) Ltd.

Proofreader: Scott Oney

Indexer: Will Ragsdale

Cover Designer: Anupama Krishnan

Marketing Manager: Nicole Elliott

Copyright © 2014 by SAGE Publications, Inc.

All rights reserved. No part of this book may be reproduced or utilized in any form or by any means, electronic or mechanical, including photocopying, recording, or by any information storage and retrieval system, without permission in writing from the publisher.

Photos on pages 68, 183, 233–235, 237–240 are from Cerf, M., Harel, J., Einhaeuser, W., & Koch, C. (2007). Predicting human gaze using low-level saliency combined with face detection. In Advances in Neural Information Processing Systems (NIPS), (vol. 20, pp. 241–248). Cambridge, MA: MIT Press.

A catalog record of this book is available from the Library of Congress.

ISBN: 978-14522-55408

BIRMINGHAM CITY UNIVERSITY

Book n: 3565 7650

Subject r: 300.285 Mad

LIBRARY

This book is printed on acid-free paper.

Certified Chain of Custody

SUSTAINABLE FORESTRY INITIATIVE

Promoting Sustainable Forestry

www.sfiprogram.org

SFI-01268

SFI label applies to text stock

13 14 15 16 17 10 9 8 7 6 5 4 3 2 1

CONTENTS

PREFACE

Behavioral research is changing. As data analysis methods change and become more computational than before, we need to change how we work as well. Nearly gone are the days when analyses can be computed by pencil, paper, and calculator, as we now enter the age of high-level computing.

My name is Christopher Madan, and I am currently a Psychology PhD candidate at the University of Alberta. Prior to beginning my graduate studies, I had been a freelance programmer for a number of years. When I first became involved in research I quickly found that learning MATLAB would be essential for the data analyses required for my work. Even though I had not used MATLAB before I became a researcher, I found that MATLAB was built for complex computations, and that it was an infinitely more efficient analysis environment than Microsoft Excel or IBM SPSS. While these other programs have their uses, MATLAB was to become the core environment for my analyses. Of course, this was in no small part based on what some of my supervisors and colleagues also used.

While I found that I was able to pick up the "logic" of MATLAB quite readily, this was likely due to my prior experience in programming. On the other hand, many of my colleagues without prior programming background have struggled to initially grasp *how* to translate their conceptual ideas of what they want to analyze into terms that MATLAB can carry out. The aim of this book is to help teach people how to do simple analyses in MATLAB and to develop a foundation for the technical skills required to conduct behavioral research.

In this book, I adopt a strong "learning by doing" approach, where I will present a data set and a problem, and then work with you to solve this problem. At the end of each chapter, I will then give you a set of similar problems for you to try and solve yourself, with the solutions included at the end of the book. Toward the end of the book, I will also present several new data sets and accompanying exercises, to allow you the space to explore your newly acquired skills but still provide a final touch of guidance to show you the breadth and flexibility that MATLAB can offer you. To this end, I would also suggest that, if possible, you work through this book with a friend. Everyone has his or her own learning style and competencies, and some topics that you may find challenging may come naturally to a colleague, and vice versa. Having someone to work with may make all the difference and save you a series of frustrated nights when you just needed a nudge in the right direction.

While my own field is experimental psychology/cognitive neuroscience, I have written this book in a manner that would hopefully help researchers in any field of behavioral research. Nonetheless, this book can also be used as an introductory primer to MATLAB, without any desire to do behavioral research, and possibly even as a general introduction to the basics of programming.

Before we begin, I would first like to thank my family as well as my colleagues at the University of Alberta and University Medical Center Hamburg-Eppendorf for their support. I would especially like to thank Yvonne Chen for her endless encouragement and suggestions, as well as Eric Legge and Jean-François Nankoo for their feedback on an earlier draft of the book. I would also like to thank Leanna Cruikshank and Mayank Rehani, without whom I never would have realized how much this book was needed. Last but not least, I'd like to thank Jeremy Caplan for first exposing me to research, and to MATLAB.

An accompanying website at www.sagepub.com/madan includes a number of datasets for use with this book.

—Christopher R. Madan

Acknowledgments

SAGE and the author gratefully acknowledge the feedback provided by the following reviewers:

Britt Anderson, University of Waterloo
Jake Clements, SUNY Geneseo
Ione Fine, University of Washington
Alen Hajnal, PhD, University of Southern Mississippi
Joseph G. Johnson, Miami University
Frank Schieber, University of South Dakota
Paul R. Schrater, University of Minnesota
Thomas Serre, Brown University
Arthur G. Shapiro, American University
Pascal Wallisch, New York University

About the Author

Christopher R. Madan is a PhD candidate (PhD expected in April 2014) in the Department of Psychology at the University of Alberta, Edmonton, Alberta, Canada. His research focuses on human memory, where he utilizes a variety of approaches, including behavioral, neuroimaging, mathematical modeling, and psychophysiology. Over the past few years he has published a number of papers, with an emphasis on the influences of emotion, reward, and movement on memory. He also often lectures on these topics, particularly on the effects of emotion on memory, cognitive neuroscience, and mathematical models of memory.

1

THE BASICS

Before we learn to ride a bicycle (without immediately falling over), we need to realize that we need to peddle. In MATLAB, there are a few things just as crucial that we need to know before we can go on our merry way.

1.1 What Is MATLAB?

MATLAB stands for **MAT**rix **LAB**oratory and is developed by MathWorks Inc.(`http://www.mathworks.com`). The key strength of MATLAB is its ability to allow you to easily work with large data sets and plot them, as well as implement complex functions for analysis and modelling. In short, MATLAB is specifically designed to simplify the execution of complex numerical computations.

1.1.1 Why Use MATLAB for Behavioral Research?

Unless you are learning MATLAB simply because your course instructor or research supervisor asked you to, you are probably wondering *why* you should do your data analyses in MATLAB, as opposed to Microsoft Excel[®] or IBM SPSS[®]. While these programs are definitely useful tools for any behavioral researcher, they are more graphically oriented, they are less effective when running multistep analyses, or even the same analysis repetitively (e.g., averaging performance across trials of the same condition, within a participant, followed by collapsed across participants for statistical comparisons). MATLAB is also particularly good at generating publication-ready figures with little manual effort. With MATLAB, you can easily adjust all of a figure's settings through commands, rather than manually every time you want to make a new figure.

With the addition of third-party toolboxes (overviewed in Section 9.2.3), you will also be able to conduct analyses that are simply not possible with Excel and SPSS, such as circular statistics, conducting mathematical modelling simulations, and analyzing neuroimaging data. You can use MATLAB to conduct experiments and collect data, but now we are getting a bit ahead of ourselves. You will likely experience a steeper learning curve with MATLAB than with Excel or SPSS, but as you advance in your career either as an academic or in industry, being able to easily work with large data sets will prove to be a useful skill. Moreover, even though MATLAB does have a steep learning curve, this can be softened dramatically if you learn MATLAB through a "problem-driven" approach, rather than just learning its various functions abstractly. In this regard, the book you are holding in your hands right now will serve as your faithful companion as you begin to learn how to use MATLAB for behavioral research.

1.2 Before We Begin

Before we begin, let's make sure you get started on the right foot. MATLAB primarily uses a command line interface, where you type in what you want to do using the MATLAB programming language. However, MATLAB also has a graphical user interface (GUI) with a handful of windows, including the command window, command history, and many others.

1.2.1 Desktop Layout

Your default desktop layout of the MATLAB GUI should be similar to Figure 1.1. As you become better acquainted with MATLAB, you may choose to modify this layout to your personal preferences. To enable/disable windows in MATLAB, click "Desktop" in the top menubar and select the name of the window you wish to add/remove. However, if you happen to accidentally close some of the windows, you can quickly reset the desktop layout by going to "Desktop" in the top menubar and choosing "Default" (see Figure 1.2).

1.2.2 Copying and Pasting Text

On Windows and Mac machines, copy and paste work in MATLAB as you would expect. In Windows, you can use CTRL+C and CTRL+V, respectively. In Mac, you can use ⌘+C and ⌘+V (⌘ is the COMMAND/APPLE key).

Figure 1.1. MATLAB default desktop layout.

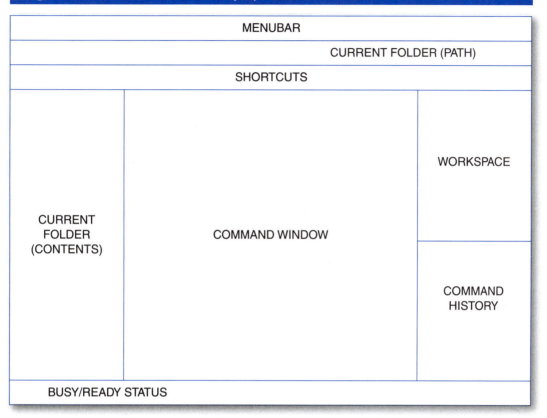

| MENUBAR |
| CURRENT FOLDER (PATH) |
| SHORTCUTS |

| CURRENT FOLDER (CONTENTS) | COMMAND WINDOW | WORKSPACE |
| | | COMMAND HISTORY |

BUSY/READY STATUS

Figure 1.2. Resetting the desktop layout.

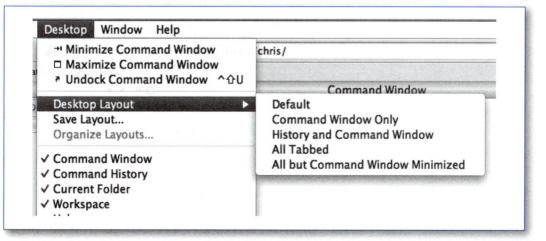

In Linux (e.g., Ubuntu, Debian, CentOS), things are a bit different. Here, the default is set to "MATLAB standard (Emacs)", and copy and paste will instead use ALT+W and CTRL+Y, respectively, which most users will not be used to. To change this, go to the "Preferences" window, which can be accessed through the "File" in the top menubar. You can then access the "Command window key bindings" section under "Keyboard". I would suggest you change this setting to "Windows" (or "Mac"), depending on what type of keyboard you are using.

1.3 Manually Entering Data

With that settled, let's get started! Let's orient ourselves to the MATLAB interface and try getting some raw data into MATLAB.

When MATLAB is ready for a command from you, it will display $>>$ in the Command Window. This is your prompt to give MATLAB some time to calculate.

Let's start with something simple.

```
1 >> 1 + 1
2 ans =
3     2
```

See, that wasn't so bad!

> ★ TIP #1
>
> If you don't tell MATLAB what to store the answer of the calculation as, it temporarily stores it as `ans`. Generally, avoid using ans in your own commands though, as its contents are constantly overwritten as you work, making it unreliable to base your code around. ∎

Rather than giving you arbitrary data to enter, let's start with a concrete example from a published study. Briefly, this data set consists of the IQ (intelligence quotient) and brain size from a sample of university students, to test if the two measures are correlated. Specifically, does a larger brain correspond to a higher IQ? In this study, Willerman, Schultz, Rutledge, and Bigler (1991) had 40 introductory psychology students complete an IQ test. (See References section at the end of the book for the full reference.) Participants who scored relatively high (IQ > 130) or relatively low (IQ < 103) on the IQ test were then invited to return for a second session where images of their brain were collected with an MRI (magnetic resonance imaging) scanner. From the MRI image, researchers deleted portions of the image that corresponded to skull and other brain coverings, leaving only portions of the image (i.e., pixels) that corresponded to brain matter. Individual brain size was then calculated as the summed area of the images that corresponded to the participants' brains. After controlling for participants' gender and body size (both height and weight), the researchers found a significant relationship between IQ and brain size. For now, we will manually type in the IQ and brain sizes for the 10 participants, just so we start getting used to MATLAB. In Chapter 2, we will learn to load the data files in directly.

To enter this series of data as a single variable, we need to use square brackets around the list of values ([ ]), separate the values with commas (,), and store the list as the variable iq (and not in ans) by using an = sign. To do this, type

```
1 >> iq = [133,140,139,133,137,99,138,92,89,133]
2 iq =
3     133   140   139   133   137   99   138   92   89   133
```

Okay, so now we have a *row* of values in MATLAB, stored in a variable called iq. Spaces can also be used instead of commas. However, if we want to store the values in a *column* instead, we can use semicolons (;).

```
1  >> iq = [133 140 139 133 137 99 138 92 89 133]
2  iq =
3      133    140    139    133    137     99    138     92     89    133
4  >> iq2 = [133;140;139;133;137;99;138;92;89;133]
5  iq2 =
6      133
7      140
8      139
9      133
10     137
11      99
12     138
13      92
14      89
15     133
```

I find code easier to read if spaces are used instead of commas, but they are both equivalent, and you can even use both commas and spaces together. Nonetheless, in this book, I will use only spaces from this point forward as I find that this makes the code look cleaner.

```
1 >> iq = [133, 140, 139, 133, 137, 99, 138, 92, 89, 133]
2 iq =
3    133   140   139   133   137    99   138    92    89   133
```

★ **TIP #2**

You can also write MATLAB code in another text editor (e.g., Notepad) and then paste it into MATLAB's command window. In Chapter 5, we'll learn to automate commands. ■

If we want to define a variable that equals a single value, we don't need square brackets. Let's set **brain** to be the value of just the first participant's brain size (units are number of pixels corresponding to brain volume from the MRI).

```
1 >> brain = 816932
2 brain =
3      816932
```

Let's now input the data for the same 10 subjects' brain sizes as a variable called **brain**.

```
1 >> brain = [ 816932 1001121 1038437 965353 951545 928799 991305 854258 ...
2 904858 955466 ]
3 brain =
4    Columns 1 through 5
5       816932      1001121      1038437       965353       951545
6    Columns 6 through 10
7       928799       991305       854258       904858       955466
```

★ **TIP #3**

You can use . . . when a line of code is long and you want to continue on the next line. ■

We can also use the square brackets ([ ]) to combine variables (concatenate). For example, you can combine the data for IQ and brain sizes into one variable, such that one continues after the other.

```
 1 >> iqbrain = [ iq brain ]
 2 iqbrain =
 3    Columns 1 through 5
 4           133           140          139          133          137
 5    Columns 6 through 10
 6            99           138           92           89          133
 7    Columns 11 through 15
 8        816932       1001121      1038437       965353       951545
 9    Columns 16 through 20
10        928799        991305       854258       904858       955466
```

With this particular set of data, that wasn't terribly useful. However, if we use both (,) *and* semicolons (;) to enter a variable, we can construct a two-dimensional matrix of values, such that each column represents one participant's IQ and brain size. Let's call this iqbrain.

```
 1 >> iqbrain = [ iq; brain ]
 2 iqbrain =
 3    Columns 1 through 5
 4           133           140          139          133          137
 5        816932       1001121      1038437       965353       951545
 6    Columns 6 through 10
 7            99           138           92           89          133
 8        928799        991305       854258       904858       955466
```

This can also be accomplished all in one step. For example, here we can make a 2 × 10 matrix that has the first row of values being the IQ scores and the second row being the brain sizes (as above).

```
 1 >> iqbrain = [133 140 139 133 137 99 138 92 89 133; ...
 2 816932 1001121 1038437 965353 951545 928799 991305 854258 ...
 3 904858 955466 ]
 4 iqbrain =
 5    Columns 1 through 5
 6           133           140          139          133          137
 7        816932       1001121      1038437       965353       951545
 8    Columns 6 through   10
 9            99           138           92           89          133
10        928799        991305       854258       904858       955466
```

Soon you will learn to

- Load data from files (p. 26)
- Plot scatterplots (p. 77)
- Calculate correlation coefficients (p. 165)

On a more general note, sometimes you need to enter a particular series of numbers that is long, but needed. Luckily, if the values in the series are sequential, MATLAB can easily take away the tedium! For example, if the series of numbers increment by one, we just need to tell MATLAB our start and end values, separated by a colon (:). (We will return to the IQ and brain-size data shortly.)

```
1 >> sub = 1:10
2 sub =
3     1    2    3    4    5    6    7    8    9    10
```

Unfortunately, our sequence seldom simply increases by a value of one. However, as long as our series of numbers increments by a constant amount, we can instead tell MATLAB the start and end values, *but* also include the increment value (and another colon) in between!

```
1 >> count = 1:0.5:4
2 count =
3    1.0000    1.5000    2.0000    2.5000    3.0000    3.5000    4.0000
4 >> count = 0:100:500
5 count =
6     0    100    200    300    400    500
7 >> count = 10:-1:1
8 count =
9    10    9    8    7    6    5    4    3    2    1
```

1.4 MATLAB Conventions

1.4.1 Semicolons

Semicolons are very important! Whenever we do a command in MATLAB, we can follow it with a semicolon (;) to suppress MATLAB from outputting the result of the command. The action still happens; we just don't need to know the result of every little thing we do. Removing these semicolons is the first thing we do when we start getting errors though!

```
1 >> sub = 1
2 sub =
3     1
4 >> sub = 1;
```

★ TIP #4

Even when the output is suppressed, commands can still affect what is stored in ans! ■

Remember, semicolons can also be used to separate rows, if used within [ ]!

Additionally, if we just type the name of a variable, we can see the data that are stored in it.

```
1 >> sub
2 sub =
3     1
```

1.4.2 Knowing Your Workspace

In MATLAB, all of the variables you store are temporarily saved in your computer's memory or MATLAB "workspace." There are a few essential functions you will need to know in order to take advantage of your workspace.

- `clear:` It clears out ALL of the variables in your workspace. This function is very useful, but be sure to use it with caution! You can try `clear sub` to clear only a specific variable (here `sub`) from the workspace.
- `clc:` It clears the command window, but keeps all of the variables. It can be quite helpful after pasting lots of code, so you can still keep track of what you're doing.
- `who:` It lists all the variables that currently exist in your workspace.

In the next chapter, we'll learn how to save your workspace for later (Section 2.9.1)!

1.5 Operating on Variables

1.5.1 Single Values

Math operations with single variables work as expected. Unfortunately, it's difficult to give concrete examples of how these operations work without a more elaborate example, so here I will use arbitrary numbers in the example.

```
 1 >> A = 2;
 2 >> B = 3;
 3 >> A + B
 4 ans =
 5       5
 6 >> A - B
 7 ans =
 8      -1
 9 >> A * B
10 ans =
11       6
12 >> A / B
13 ans =
14     0.6667
15 >> (A*A)+B
16 ans =
17       7
```

1.5.2 Integer-izing Your Values

When you have decimal numbers and you need an integer, consider one of the following: `round, floor, ceil`. Which is the best solution depends on your particular situation. Briefly, `round` rounds non-integer numbers to the nearest integer, as you would expect. `floor` will always round a number *down* to the nearest integer; `ceil` will always round a number *up* to the nearest integer.

To use these three functions, as well as almost any function in MATLAB, we type the name of the function followed by the name of the variable we want to input into that function, with that variable name surrounded by brackets (( )). For example, round(A) to use the `round` on variable A.

```
 1 >> A = 1.5;
 2 >> [ round(A) floor(A) ceil(A) ]
 3 ans =
 4      2    1    2
 5 >> B = 6.3;
 6 >> [ round(B) floor(B) ceil(B) ]
 7 ans =
 8      6    6    7
 9 >> C = 4.8;
10 >> [ round(C) floor(C) ceil(C) ]
11 ans =
12      5    4    5
```

1.6 Simple Math With Variables

Let's get started on actually working with some numbers!

1.6.1 Adding and Subtracting a Series of Values

```
1 >> A = [1 2 3];
2 >> B = [10 23 45];
3 >> A + B
4 ans =
5     11    25    48
```

Well, that made sense! Subtraction works almost identically.

```
1 >> A - B
2 ans =
3     -9    -21    -42
```

1.6.2 Multiplying and Dividing Variables

We'll use the same A and B variables for now. We can't just use * to multiply variables, as that refers to matrix algebra, and our vectors here don't match up correctly for that. (For our purposes here, a vector is simply a variable that is a series of values.) Instead we need to use .* (i.e., a period followed by an asterisk). This corresponds to so-called element-wise multiplication, where the first value in variable A is multiplied with the first value from B, the second value of A with the second value of B, and so on. Make sure you don't forget the period just before the asterisk symbol!

```
1 >> A * B
2 ??? Error using ==> mtimes
3 Inner matrix dimensions must agree.
4 >> A .* B
5 ans =
6     10     46     135
```

In regard to division, even though / does not produce an error, it is also not the function you would be looking for. As with multiplication, you need to include the period before the slash symbol: ./.

```
1 >> A / B
2 ans =
3     0.0720
4 >> A ./ B
5 ans =
6     0.1000     0.0870     0.0667
```

★ **TIP #5**

Unless you are doing linear algebra, .* and ./ are what you are looking for. ■

1.6.3 Transposing Variables

To "transpose" a row variable into a column variable (or vice versa), follow the variable's name with an apostrophe (').

```
1 >> A = [4 5 9 3]
2 A =
3     4     5     9     3
4 >> A'
5 ans =
6     4
7     5
8     9
9     3
```

Note that transposing a variable is *not* the same thing as just rotating the matrix. Transposing rotates the whole matrix along the diagonal, so the values in the first row instead becomes the values in the first column. Let's try illustrating this with the `iqbrain` variable from earlier that contained the IQ and brain-size data.

```
 1 >> iqbrain
 2 iqbrain =
 3   Columns 1 through 5
 4            133          140          139          133          137
 5         816932      1001121      1038437       965353       951545
 6   Columns 6 through 10
 7             99          138           92           89          133
 8         928799       991305       854258       904858       955466
 9 >> iqbrain'
10 ans =
11            133       816932
12            140      1001121
13            139      1038437
14            133       965353
15            137       951545
16             99       928799
17            138       991305
18             92       854258
19             89       904858
20            133       955466
```

If instead we simply rotated the data in `iqbrain`, you should have expected either

```
 1            133       955466
 2             89       904858
 3             92       854258
 4            138       991305
 5             99       928799
 6            137       951545
 7            133       965353
 8            139      1038437
 9            140      1001121
10            133       816932
```

or

```
1   Columns 1 through 5
2       955466        904858         854258         991305         928799
3          133            89             92            138             99
4   Columns 6 through 10
5       951545        965353        1038437        1001121         816932
6          137           133            139            140            133
```

★ TIP #6

If you actually intend to rotate a matrix of values, look into `rot90`. ■

1.7 Working With Only the Data We Want

When we have a matrix with many values, sometimes we just need to call a subset of the data. Usually this means looking up a single value, a single row/column, a combination of several rows/columns, or only certain dimensions of the data set.

For starters, given a two-dimensional matrix of data, the data are basically arranged in a grid, with the first "dimension" being the row number and the second dimension being the column number.

This would be a great time to return to our `iqbrain` with IQ and brain sizes! First, let's transpose our data such that row corresponds to the IQ and brain size for an individual participant, rather than having an IQ row and a brain-size row.

```
 1  >> iqbrain = iqbrain'
 2  Iqbrain =
 3            133        816932
 4            140       1001121
 5            139       1038437
 6            133        965353
 7            137        951545
 8             99        928799
 9            138        991305
10             92        854258
11             89        904858
12            133        955466
```

Isn't that easier to look at than before?

Next, we need to be able to only call specific values from the data. To obtain the whole range for that dimension, we simply use a colon (:). To obtain specific subsets of the dimension, create a variable to describe the subset you want—either by listing values contained in square brackets ([ ]) or by creating a variable with the start and end values, separated by a colon (:). You can also use **end** to represent the last "row" or "column" number. For this example, let's use the variable we already have named iqbrain.

First, let's try and retrieve only the IQ scores, which should be stored in the first row of iqbrain, and then both the IQ and brain size for the third participant.

```
 1 >> iqbrain(:,1)
 2 ans =
 3      133
 4      140
 5      139
 6      133
 7      137
 8       99
 9      138
10       92
11       89
12      133
13 >> iqbrain(3,:)
14 ans =
15           139        1038437
```

Importantly, the first position specifies the row, and the second specifies the column. Also, note that the indexes in MATLAB start from 1. While this may seem intuitive for those without programming experience, this is important to point out as numerous other programming languages use 0 as the first index.

Also, remember that variable names in MATLAB *are* case sensitive. If you forget, you will get an error. Or, worse yet, the *wrong* value if you happened to have another variable named IQBrain, though that is generally a bad idea anyway.

```
 1 >> IQBrain(3,:)
 2 ??? Undefined variable IQBrain.
```

Let's try and extract a few more specific values from this data set: the brain size for participant 5, the IQ score for participants 8 through 10, and the brain sizes for participants 4 and 7.

```
 1 >> iqbrain(5,2)
 2 ans =
 3        951545
 4 >> iqbrain(8:10,1)
 5 ans =
 6      92
 7      89
 8     133
 9 >> iqbrain([4 7],2)
10 ans =
11        965353
12        991305
```

Notice that to get the IQs for participants 8 through 10 we made a vector that contains the values [8 9 10] using 8:10. Similarly, to get the brain sizes for participants 4 and 7, we had to make a vector using the square brackets ([ ]). Without these brackets, MATLAB will not understand what we want to do and will instead produce an error.

```
 1 >> 8:10
 2 ans =
 3       8        9       10
 4 >> [4 7]
 5 ans =
 6       4        7
 7 >> 4 7
 8 ??? 4 7
 9          |
10 Error: Unexpected MATLAB expression.
```

★ TIP #7

There is no reason we should be confined to two-dimensional matrices. For example, if we had IQ and brain-size data for a second group of participants, such as a sample of older adults, we could append it to what we already have and make a three-dimensional variable. Don't worry about this for now; it's just something to keep in mind. ■

Let's try one more thing: What if we want to replace the values in a specific index of a variable, such as if we noticed a typo. Let's try and set the brain size for participant 9 to "100," and then set it back to its original value—as the value is currently correct. We can change the value in a particular index simply by specifying the index we want to change and then using = to tell MATLAB what we want to change it to.

```
 1 >> iqbrain(9,2)
 2 ans =
 3        904858
 4 >> iqbrain(9,2) = 100
 5 iqbrain =
 6             133        816932
 7             140       1001121
 8             139       1038437
 9             133        965353
10             137        951545
11              99        928799
12             138        991305
13              92        854258
14              89           100
15             133        955466
16 >> iqbrain(9,2) = 904858
17 iqbrain =
18             133        816932
19             140       1001121
20             139       1038437
21             133        965353
22             137        951545
23              99        928799
24             138        991305
25              92        854258
26              89        904858
27             133        955466
```

★ TIP #8

To modify the contents of a variable more interactively, you can also use the `openvar` function, which can open a window that lets you edit the contents of a variable. This window can also be opened by double-clicking on a variable in the Workspace pane in the MATLAB GUI. ■

1.8 Calling It a Day

We can't end the chapter before you know how to close MATLAB, right? While you can simply click the "×" to close MATLAB, just like any other program, you probably also want to know how to close it with commands. To close MATLAB, just type `exit` or `quit`.

If you close MATLAB unintentionally, you will lose all of the variables you had stored in memory! To prevent this from happening by accident, go to

File > Preferences > General > Confirmation Dialogs and check the box beside "Confirm before exiting MATLAB". When you're just getting used to MATLAB, having to click this button before quitting is a small price to pay for an added margin of safety!

1.9 The End of the Beginning

Okay, so we know how to enter variables into MATLAB and do some simple operations on them . . . nothing to call home about. That's okay, this was *just* Chapter 1. Let's try and make Chapter 2 a bit more productive, shall we?

The best way to learn a skill is through practice. To try and help you along, I've included a few exercises, along with their solutions in the back of this book. I hope they help!

EXERCISES

Using the *final version* variable that we created called iqbrain that had a row for each participant (a 2 ×10 matrix), answer the following questions:

1. What was the IQ for participant 10?

2. What were the brain sizes for participants 1 to 3?

3. What were the IQ and brain size for participants 5 and 9?

4. What was the average IQ for participants 1 to 3? (Try your best for now; we will learn better ways to average numbers in Section 3.2.)

5. Find the average brain size for participants 8 and 10.

6. Divide participant 7's brain size by her IQ.

7. Divide the IQ for all 10 participants by their corresponding brain size.

See page 191 for the solutions. Hopefully that wasn't too difficult. We're only getting started!

FUNCTION REVIEW

Operators: `[ ] , : ; ( ) .* ./ '`

General: `ans clear clc who`

Rounding: `round floor ceil`

Exiting: `end exit quit`

2

Data, Meet MATLAB

In Chapter 1, you had to input the sample data by hand. Obviously, we can't carry on like that for too long, so it's time we learn to work with functions, as well as how to import existing data into MATLAB and get data out of MATLAB.

2.1 Functions

Before we begin, we need to learn a little bit about "functions." A function is a series of MATLAB commands that are written and saved as a single file so that they can easily be executed. For now, we will will learn to use a few MATLAB functions, and in Section 5.8, we will learn to make our own functions.

> ★ **TIP #9**
>
> "Directory" is another name for a "folder." ■

Briefly, to access files on your computer, regardless of operating system, your computer has a "directory structure," where directories are nested within each other to better organize your files. For instance, your Desktop folder is usually found inside a directory that has your user-specific files. This user folder also contains your Documents ("My Documents") folder, along with a folder for your music files. The *path* to the music files on your machine would include your user folder, the Music folder, and then maybe the artist and album name that the music file came from.

2.2 Paths

To access functions in MATLAB, they need to be in a specific directory. All functions that are part of MATLAB are already included and ready to use. However, if we want to add any of our own, such as those that came with this book, we need to put them in the right place.

If we type `path` in MATLAB, it will list out all of the directories on your computer where MATLAB functions are being stored that are readily accessible.

```
 1  >> path
 2          MATLABPATH
 3      /Users/chris/matlab
 4      /Users/chris/Documents/matlab
 5      /Applications/MATLAB.app/toolbox/matlab/general
 6      /Applications/MATLAB.app/toolbox/matlab/ops
 7      /Applications/MATLAB.app/toolbox/matlab/lang
 8      /Applications/MATLAB.app/toolbox/matlab/elmat
 9      /Applications/MATLAB.app/toolbox/matlab/randfun
10      ...
```

This list can be quite long, so I only included the first few entries in the example.

2.2.1 Your Personal Function Folder

Most of those folders listed are in the main folder where MATLAB itself is, and you probably don't want to put your "personal" functions there. To accommodate this, MATLAB automatically adds two folders specific to you when it loads, but only if these folders already exist. The location of this folder varies based on what operating system you use and is always relative to your "user folder." Since Windows, Mac OS X, and Linux all use different folder structures, this gets a bit messy. The location of your user folder should be the following, based on your operating system; here are examples based on my own username:

Windows Path: `C:\Users\Chris\`

Mac OS X Path: `/Users/chris/`

Linux Path: `/home/chris/`

Conveniently, ~ ("tilde") can be used to denote the user folder in Mac OS X and Linux (as they are all based on a common precursor operating system). This can be particularly useful when navigating through the files and folders on our computer. Windows users, don't fret, the function covered in next section should remedy this well enough.

Now that we know where your user folder is, let's head over to your personal MATLAB folder. This folder can be in one of two places.

Folder 1: Directly in your user directory

Path: ~\matlab\

Folder 2: In your documents

Windows Path: ~\My Documents\matlab\

Mac OS X and Linux Path: ~/Documents/matlab/

> **★ TIP #10**
>
> If you're unsure where your own MATLAB function folder is, use userpath to check. ∎

Now that we know where we should put our personal functions, this would be a good time to download the files that go along with this book from http://www.sagepub.com/madan/ and unzip them. For the rest of the book, the examples will assume that you extracted the files into a folder called "matlabintro" on your Desktop.

Now, you should copy the files from the book files' functions folder to your own personal function folder. To test if this worked properly, type imbwelcome in MATLAB.

```
1 >> imbwelcome
2 Congratulations, you have successfully installed the MATLAB functions
3 from "An Introduction to MATLAB for Behavioral Researchers."
```

For your convenience, all of the functions that come with this book are prefixed with "imb."

2.2.2 You Are Here

While you can access MATLAB functions, and now the functions that came with this book, from anywhere, you will want them to be in a specific folder when you do your analyses. Specifically, when you want to save figures or output text files from MATLAB, you don't want them to just be saved anywhere on your computer. However, before we can tell MATLAB where we *want* to be, we must first find out where we are in the first place. MATLAB has a function for this specific purpose, called **pwd** or 'present working directory'.

```
1 >> pwd
2 ans =
3 /Users/chris/Documents/matlab/
```

We can also get MATLAB to list the contents of the current folder, using **dir** and **ls**.

```
 1 >> ls
 2 fillPage.m              imbspear.m           imbwelcome.m
 3 fillPage_license.txt    imbtcdf.m            randblock.m
 4 imbcorr.m               imbtinv.m            randblock_license.txt
 5 imbhex2color.m          imbttest.m
 6 imbmatlab2txt.m         imbttest2.m
 7 >> dir
 8 .                       imbhex2color.m       imbttest2.m
 9 ..                      imbmatlab2txt.m      imbwelcome.m
10 .DS_Store               imbspear.m           randblock.m
11 fillPage.m              imbtcdf.m            randblock_license.txt
12 fillPage_license.txt    imbtinv.m
13 imbcorr.m               imbttest.m
```

2.3 A New Type of Variable: Strings

In Chapter 1, we only dealt with one "type" of variable: numbers. (For the more programming inclined among you, there are different types of number variables in MATLAB, but we won't worry about that for now.) However, you may have noticed that when we use **pwd**, MATLAB returns the path to the current directory through **ans**. This is because the output of the function **pwd** is a *string* of characters.

```
1 >> here = pwd
2 here =
3 /Users/chris/Documents/matlab
```

In a string, each letter has its own index.

```
1 >> here(1:15)
2 ans =
3 /Users/chris/Do
4 >> here(20:end)
5 ans =
6 nts/matlab
```

We can also make our own strings, using *single quotes*.

```
1 >> string = 'This is my first string!'
2 string =
3 This is my first string!
4 >> hello = 'Hello MATLAB!'
5 hello =
6 Hello MATLAB!
```

You're probably wondering, "Why learn about strings right now?" Well, to tell MATLAB the path to the folder with our data, we have to be able to tell MATLAB the folder names as *strings*. Later in the book, we will also learn to use strings to set up our figure. In particular, the title of the figure and axis labels need to be defined as strings, but they can also come in handy in other instances. We will discuss making figures in Chapter 4.

2.4 Navigating Directories

Now that we know where we are, we need to think about where we *want* to be, such as a folder with the data from our experiment.

2.4.1 The GUI Way

One way to navigate to another folder in MATLAB is through the GUI (graphical user interface). At the top of the MATLAB window, there is a section called "current directory" (see Figure 2.1). Here MATLAB tells us where we are, similarly to `pwd`, but also has a button labelled as ". . .". If we click this button, a dialog box pops up that lets us navigate to where we want to be, just like in any other program.

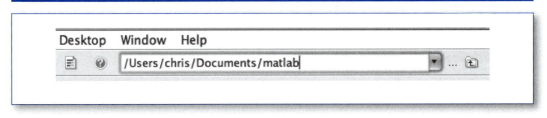

Figure 2.1   Changing your working directory in MATLAB using the GUI.

2.4.2 The Command Line Way

While navigating to another folder via the GUI works great, nearly everything we do in MATLAB is done by commands. In the long run, it will actually be more convenient to get around using MATLAB commands. To do this, we use the cd command or 'change directory'. Type cd('..') to go up a directory. Below is an example of how to navigate between the folders.

```
1 >> cd('../..')
2 >> dir
3 Applications    Downloads    Movies      Public
4 Desktop    Library    Music        Sites
5 Documents    MATLAB      Pictures
6 >> cd('Desktop/matlabintro/')
7 >> pwd
8 ans =
9 /Users/chris/Desktop/matlabintro
```

Notice that you can put multiple folder changes together!

Note, though, that MATLAB will also let you type the same commands without the brackets and single quotes (as shown below). However, most MATLAB functions do not allow this, so I will always use brackets for consistency.

```
1 >> cd('../..')
2 >> cd('Desktop/matlabintro')
```

2.4.3 Returning Home

Now that you can adventure around the file structure of your computer, it may also be helpful to quickly return to your home directory. As mentioned earlier, MATLAB interprets "~" as the path of your user/home directory on Mac OS X and Linux machines.

```
1 >> cd('~')
2 >> pwd
3 ans =
4 /Users/chris
```

★ TIP #11

You can also go to paths relative to your home directory. For example, try "~/Desktop". ∎

2.5 Press TAB to Complete

Now that you're typing names of variables, variables, and directory paths, you might get irritated that some of them are just too long! Rather than reorganizing all of your folders, though this might also be worth considering, we will learn to easily autocomplete typing of long names. Just type the first few letters of the name, and then press the "TAB" key on your keyboard. MATLAB will automatically complete the rest of the name, if there is only one possible solution. If there are multiple completions and MATLAB is unsure what the correct completion is, a yellow pop-up window will appear (see Figure 2.2). Here, you can either continue to type the name or you can navigate through this list with the arrow keys and press the "ENTER" key to select it.

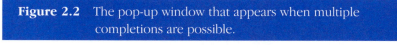

Figure 2.2   The pop-up window that appears when multiple completions are possible.

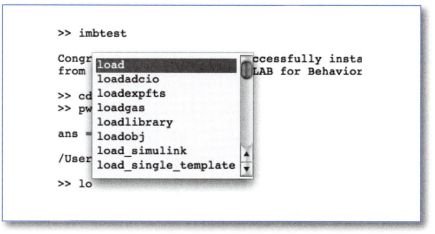

> ★ **TIP #12**
>
> Using the up and down arrows, you can also cycle through previous commands. If you type the first few characters, you can narrow your search to only previous commands that match the same first characters. ∎

2.6 Opening Data Files

Before we can do any analyses, we need to first get our data into MATLAB. Now that we can navigate to the folder with our data, we need to know how to open our data files in the MATLAB workspace. There are several ways to do this, such as `load`, `dlmread`, or `textscan`, or we can work with files more directly.

2.6.1 Using `load`

`load` is MATLAB's principle function for loading data. Data can be a text file with columns of data separated by tabs or commas, or it can be MATLAB's own `.mat` file format, which we will learn to make in the next section.

Let's give this a try using some of the sample data provided with this book.

```
 1 >> cd('~/Desktop/matlabintro')
 2 >> ls
 3 data            functions
 4 >> cd('data')
 5 >> dir
 6 2dpeck      decision1   demo        iqbrain
 7 bristol     decision2   eyetrack    worddb
 8 >> cd('iqbrain')
 9 >> ls
10 data.txt        data_legend.txt     datawheaders.txt
11 >> load('data.txt')
```

When you use `load`, data gets stored in a variable named after the file it was loaded from. In this case, it is called `data`. Of course, you can alternatively specify the name of the variable that you want to store the data as.

```
1 >> iqbrain = load('data.txt')
```

If you take a look at the data stored in `iqbrain`, you will see that it is the same data we used in Chapter 1, but with additional columns and more participants. Details on each column can be found in `data_legend.txt`. At the time I figured that IQ and brain size (the main measures) for 10 participants was enough for you to enter manually. Also note that there are a few instances where values are missing and the file instead has a "NaN" marked; don't worry about them for now, but we'll learn about those in Section 3.8.

> **★ TIP #13**
>
> Some functions can also be accessed in other ways. For example, you can also type "`load data.txt`", without using any brackets or quotation marks. However, most functions do not work this way. For consistency, I will always use brackets in the examples. ■

2.6.2 Using `dlmread`

Sometimes we need a bit more control than `load` will give us, for example, if there is extra text at the beginning of the file—such as the column headers. Additionally, the main difference between `dlmread` and `load` is evident in the function's name: `dlmread` can "read" files that use any specified "delimiter," that is, what character(s) separate the columns. If we do not specify a particular delimiter, the `dlmread` functions similar to `load`.

`dlmread` is our first function where we can input multiple parameters, separated by commas. Here we can specify the file name with the data we want to import into MATLAB, the column delimiter we want to use, and the row and column that we want to start reading the file from. Unlike most of the rest of MATLAB, the row and column indices used in `dlmread` count starting from zero. Incorporating these parameters, we would use the function as `dlmread(filename, delimiter, first row, first column)`.

To try this with actual data, we can try to read in a version of the IQ and brain-size data that has the column headers, but we can skip over these lines.

```
1 >> dlmread('datawheaders.txt', ' ', 1 ,0)
```

With this command, we loaded the data from file "datawheaders.txt", using a space as the delimiter, and starting with the second row and first column.

2.6.3 Using `textscan`

While `load` and `dlmread` can work well for a wide variety of data files, they will fail miserably if your data have `text` in it directly (i.e., not just in the headers).

> **★ TIP #14**
>
> Using `textscan` can be a bit daunting at first. Feel free to skip over this part for now and come back later. ■

Let's try this out right now, and then we'll learn to import data into MATLAB using another function, `textscan`. Leave the `iqbrain` directory and instead go to the one called `worddb`. The data here are from another study, one where the researchers constructed a word database (hence "worddb").

In this study, Janschewitz (2008) had 85 students at a U.S. university rate a large sample of words (460 words) on a number of scales, with the intention that future studies could then use this normed database to design studies with better-controlled stimuli. Specifically, these words were positive-valenced emotional words (e.g., cake, erotic, profit), negative-valenced (e.g., dirt, horror, roach) taboo words, or emotionally neutral. Separate emotionally neutral words were selected as either being part of a general word category (relating to household objects) or being unrelated. Both positive and negative words were also subdivided into being relatively higher or lower in emotional arousal, making for a total of seven word types. The main focus of this word database was the inclusion of taboo words, such that they can be better matched to other words in future studies. (See Janschewitz, 2008, if you are interested in more details regarding the word selection/study motivation.)

Participants rated each of these 460 words on seven different scales. Each scale ranged from 1 to 9, with 9 being the highest possible rating. The seven scales were as follows: (1) *Personal use*, how often the participant used a word. (2) *Familiarity*, how often the participant heard/read the word. (3) *Offensiveness*, how offensive/upsetting the word was to the participant. (4) *Tabooness*, how offensive/upsetting the participant thought the word was to people in general. (5) *Valence*, how positive or negative (i.e., good vs. bad) the participant found the word (9 = extremely positive). A rating of 5 here would imply that the word was neither particularly positive nor particularly negative. (6) *Arousal*, how exciting or attention grabbing a word was. (7) *Imageability*, how easy it was to form a mental image of the word. (For the exact phrasing of these scales, see Appendix A of Janschewitz, 2008.) In addition to the these ratings, the word database from Janschewitz (2008) also included the number of letters and syllables in each word, the word frequency (how common a word is in the English language [per million words], as calculated in a prior database, when available; "K&F - Freq."), and the valence and arousal ratings from another prior database (when available; "ANEW - Valence" and "ANEW - Arousal").

Okay, now that we know what the data are about, let's try and open it up in MATLAB! If we were to just try using load, let's see what happens.

```
1 >> load('JanschewitzB386appB.txt')
2 ??? Error using ==> load
3 Number of columns on line 1 of ASCII file
4 /Users/chris/Desktop/matlabintro/data/worddb/JanschewitzB386appB,txt
5 must be the same as previous lines.
```

As you can see, that didn't work very well. The problem is that the text file contains a fair amount of text, and MATLAB isn't sure how to read the file in properly. Before we go any further, let's open the file ouselves so we have a better idea of what we're working with. Skimming through the file should look like this:

```
1 Appendix B
2 Word Ratings and Associated Statistics (All Participants)
3
4 Word    Type       Letters Syllables  K&F    ANEW                 Per...
5                                        Freq.  Valence  Arousal    Mean
6 ...
7 angel   pos lo ar  5       2          18     7.53     4.83        4.25
8 bath    pos lo ar  4       1          26     7.33     4.16        4.86
9 beauty  pos lo ar  6       2          71     7.82     4.95        5.96
10 ...
11 alone   neg lo ar  5       2          195    2.41     4.83        5.55
12 blister neg lo ar  7       2          3      2.88     4.10        3.71
13 broken  neg lo ar  6       2          63     3.05     5.43        5.51
14 ...
15 aloof   unrel neu  5       2          5      4.90     4.28        3.00
16 ankle   unrel neu  5       2          8      5.27     4.16        4.87
17 arm     unrel neu  3       1          94     5.34     3.59        6.00
18 ...
19 Note. Type refers to word type. Abbreviations: pos lo ar = positive...
20 arousal; unrel neu = category-unrelated neutral; rel neu = category...
21 ratings from Bradley & Lang's (1999) Affective Norms for English Words
```

(The lines are too long to fit on the page here, so only the first few columns are shown.)

Hopefully, the data set makes a bit more sense now. The taboo words are listed first, as that was how the text file was provided from the Janschewitz (2008) study, but we'll try and not focus on the taboo words themselves too much. To open this data in MATLAB, we will need to take a more basic, hands-on approach than we did with `load` and `dlmread`. Here we will open the file, then read its contents, and last close the file.

To open and close the file, we will use the functions **fopen** and **fclose**, while assigning a file ID to the file when we open it. These functions work at a relatively low level in MATLAB, so we won't get into their details in this book, but feel free to look over the help documentation by typing help('`fopen`'). As a quick example, let's try and just open and close a text file, without doing anything with it just yet.

```
1 >> fid = fopen('JanschewitzB386appB.txt','r');
2 >> fclose(fid);
```

Now, opening and then closing a file is pretty pointless unless we do something in the middle, right? We just did that first so we had that part down, before things get a bit more complicated.

Before we can read in the text file using **textscan**, we need to be ready to tell MATLAB which columns are text ('%s,'s is for strings) and which are numbers ('%f,' a type of number format in MATLAB). If we look again at the columns in our file, we would see that the first two are the only ones with text in them, and the rest are all numbers. Given that there are 21 columns in total, that would mean we have 19 columns of numbers (feel free to double-check this yourself!). To make the variable that defines which columns are strings and which are numbers, we need to make a string that is a list of '%s's and '%f's. If we had two columns of strings followed by only three columns of numbers, we could just do this:

```
1 >> formatstring = '%s %s %f %f %f';
```

Unfortunately, we have 19 columns of numbers and I don't think either of us want to type out "%f" exactly 19 times. Thankfully, we can get MATLAB to take care of this for us using the **repmat** function. The **repmat** function **rep**eats a **mat**rix a set number of times, either as repeating columns or as rows. `repmat` takes three inputs: first, the value we want to repeat, followed by the number of times the matrix should be repeated in the row dimension, and then the number of repeats in the column dimension. For instance, if our original value was only one row, giving `repmat` inputs of 5 and 1 as the latter two values, we would get an output matrix with 5 rows.

```
1 >> in = 123;
2 >> repmat(in,5,1)
3 ans =
4      123
5      123
6      123
7      123
8      123
```

Before heading straight into our 19 repeating characters, let's test the `repmat` function out a bit more. If we want to repeat a string five times, in the row direction, we just change what's stored in our **in** variable.

```
1 >> in='test';
2 >> repmat(in,5,1)
3 ans =
4 test
5 test
6 test
7 test
8 test
```

Now, for our actual **formatstring**, we need to repeat the number portion of it 19 times and precede that with two columns for strings.

```
 1 >> repmat(' %f', 1,5)
 2 ans =
 3 %f %f %f %f %f
 4 >> repmat(' %f',1,19)
 5 ans =
 6 %f %f %f %f %f %f %f %f %f %f %f %f %f %f %f %f %f %f %f
 7 >> [ '%s %s' repmat(' %f',1,19) ]
 8 ans =
 9 %s %s %f %f %f %f %f %f %f %f %f %f %f %f %f %f %f %f %f %f %f
10 >> formatstring = [ '%s %s' repmat(' %f', 1, 19) ]
11 formatstring =
12 %s %s %f %f %f %f %f %f %f %f %f %f %f %f %f %f %f %f %f %f %f
```

Okay, we're almost ready to read in the text file. As a reminder, and for your reference, I've listed the column titles below.

```
 1 Word
 2 Type
 3 Letters
 4 Syllables
 5 K&F - Freq.
 6 ANEW - Valence
 7 ANEW - Arousal
 8 Personal Use - Mean
 9 Personal Use - SD
10 Familiarity - Mean
11 Familiarity - SD
12 Offensiveness - Mean
13 Offensiveness - SD
14 Tabooness - Mean
15 Tabooness - SD
16 Valence - Mean
17 Valence - SD
18 Arousal - Mean
19 Arousal - SD
20 Imageability - Mean
21 Imageability - SD
```

The `textscan` function, the function that actually reads the text file into a MATLAB variable, has a few important options in it, namely the number of header lines (`headerlines`) and the column delimiter (`delimiter`). To learn more about `textscan`, you can use the help functions that we will learn in Chapter 3.

★ **TIP #15**

If you don't specify a delimiter directly, `textscan` will count any white-space character as dividing the columns. ■

Note that if you make a mistake in `formatstring`, you will need to use `fopen` and `fclose` again to reopen and close the file. You will likely not get an error; MATLAB will instead have reorganized the data to fit this incorrect formatting. See an example below.

```
1 >> fid = fopen('JanschewitzB386appB.txt','r');
2 >> formatstring = [ '%s %s' repmat(' %f',1,5) ]
3 formatstring =
4 %s %s %f %f %f %f %f
```

```
 5 >> worddata=textscan(fid,formatstring,'headerlines',5, ...
 6 'delimiter','\t')
 7 worddata =
 8   Columns 1 through 4
 9     {1392x1 cell}    {1392x1 cell}    [1392x1 double]    [1392x1 double]
10   Columns 5 through 7
11     [1392x1 double]    [1392x1 double]    [1391x1 double]
12 >> fclose(fid);
```

Okay, let's do it right this time, with all 21 columns in total.

```
 1 >> fid = fopen('JanschewitzB386appB.txt','r');
 2 >> formatstring = [ '%s %s' repmat(' %f',1,19) ]
 3 'formatstring =
 4 %s %s %f %f %f %f %f %f %f %f %f %f %f %f %f %f %f %f %f %f %f
 5 >> worddata=textscan(fid,formatstring,'headerlines',5, ...
 6 'delimiter','\t')
 7 worddata =
 8   Columns 1 through 4
 9     {464x1 cell}    {464x1 cell}    [464x1 double]    [464x1 double]
10   Columns 5 through 8
11     [464x1 double]    [464x1 double]    [464x1 double]    [464x1 double]
12   Columns 9 through 12
13     [464x1 double]    [464x1 double]    [464x1 double]    [464x1 double]
14   Columns 13 through 16
15     [464x1 double]    [464x1 double]    [464x1 double]    [464x1 double]
16   Columns 17 through 20
17     [464x1 double]    [464x1 double]    [464x1 double]    [464x1 double]
18   Column 21
19     [463x1 double]
20 >> fclose(fid);
```

Okay, let's go back to when we did this correctly with the 19 number columns. There are two important things to notice: (1) The first two columns of worddata are being called cell whereas the number columns are being called double and (2) the last column (column 21) is 463 rows in length while the other 20 columns are 464 rows. Let's discuss these each in turn.

"Cell" variables are an alternative to storing text data as individual characters, where the text (i.e., word) can be stored as a single value. The cell format can also be used to store text and numbers within the same variable. We will discuss cell variables further in the next section. "Double" is another data format within MATLAB, used for numbers. In almost all cases, MATLAB will store numbers in the double format.

Let's take a look at the data in `worddata`, which is itself a cell variable.

```
1 >> worddata(1)
2 ans =
3     {463x1 cell}
```

Note that the { and } brackets keep coming up when we use cell variables. We can use these { and } brackets to access values inside a cell variable, instead of the usual (and) brackets.

```
1  >> worddata{1}
2  ans =
3      ...
4      'angel'
5      'bath'
6      'beauty'
7      ...
8      'alone'
9      'blister'
10     'broken'
11     ...
12     'aloof'
13     'ankle'
14     'arm'
15     ...
```

We probably don't want to see all the rows in `worddata` at the same time. Let's try and get MATLAB to show us only a few entries, say words 101 to 105. This works as if each column of `worddata` is its own matrix (because it kind of is).

```
1  >> worddata{1}(101:105)
2  ans =
3      'carefree'
4      'caress'
5      'color'
6      'cozy'
7      'dignified'
8  >> worddata{2}(101:105)
9  ans =
10     'pos lo ar'
11     'pos lo ar'
12     'pos lo ar'
13     'pos lo ar'
14     'pos lo ar'
```

I think that's enough of the text portion of this data for now. Don't worry, we'll revisit it again in the next chapter. If you recall, there was still one other issue: the inconsistent number of columns. The reason for this is relatively simple: If you look at the original text file, you will notice that the last few lines are some notes by the author.

```
1 Note. Type refers to word type. Abbreviations: pos lo ar = positive...
2 arousal; unrel neu = category-unrelated neutral; rel neu = category...
3 ratings from Bradley & Lang's (1999) Affective Norms for English Words
```

As you can probably figure, these last few lines don't really match up with our **formatstring** variable and make a bit more work for us in MATLAB. While I could have simply removed these lines from the text file prior to having us import it into MATLAB, I instead decided to use the file exactly as it came from the appendix of the paper and to show you a few more tricks in MATLAB. If we look at the last entries in MATLAB, we can see these end-of-file comments.

```
 1 >> worddata{1}(455:end)
 2 ans =
 3      'table'
 4      'terrace'
 5      'towel'
 6      'vase'
 7      'wash'
 8      'window'
 9      ' '
10      [1x176 char]
11      [1x168 char]
12      [1x71  char]
```

Since the actual data end at line 460 (as that's how many words there are in the database), we can simply disregard the rows that come afterward.

> **Soon you will learn to**
>
> - Calculate descriptive statistics for experimental conditions (p.46)
> - Plot bar graphs and scatterplots (pp. 67 and 77)
> - Calculate inferential statistics such as *t* tests and correlation coefficients (pp. 156 and 165)

2.7 A New Type of Variable: Cell Array

Cell arrays are kind of a combination of a regular array of numbers and a string. With an array of numbers, you can make columns and rows of values, regardless of the size of numbers; that is, you are not constrained to one digit per "index."

```
1 >> temp = 123;
2 >> temp(1)
3 ans =
4     123
5 >> temp'
6 temp =
7     123
```

With strings you can use letters, but each character has its own index. If you want to have several rows of letters (i.e., each word on its own line), you need to "pad" shorter strings with spaces so that each line is the same number of characters in length.

```
1 >> temp = 'one';
2 >> temp(1)
3 ans =
4 o
5 >> temp
6 temp =
7 one
8 >> temp(3)
9 ans =
10 e
11 >> temp'
12 ans =
13 o
14 n
15 e
```

With cell arrays, you can store strings of letters within a single cell, with each word having its own index.

```
1 >> temp = {'one'}
2 temp =
3     'one'
```

```
 4 >> temp(1)
 5 ans =
 6      'one'
 7 >> temp'
 8 ans =
 9      'one'
10 >> temp(2)
11 ??? Index exceeds matrix dimensions.
```

If we want to store multiple words together, cell variables become particularly useful. First, let's give character matrices a try for comparison.

```
 1 >> temp= [ 'one', 'two' ]
 2 temp =
 3 onetwo
 4 >> temp'
 5 ans =
 6 o
 7 n
 8 e
 9 t
10 w
11 o
12 >> temp = [ 'one'; 'two' ]
13 temp =
14 one
15 two
16 >> temp'
17 ans =
18 ot
19 nw
20 eo
21 >> temp = [ 'one'; 'two'; 'three' ]
22 ??? Error using ==> vertcat
23 CAT arguments dimensions are not consistent.
```

As you can see, strings using character matrices can kind of work when the words are of the same length, for example, "one" and "two." However, we run into problems when the words are not of the same length, for example, "three." There are some ways around this though, such as to use spaces in our strings to "pad" all of the words to be the same number of characters.

```
1 >> temp= [ 'one '; 'two '; 'three' ]
2 temp =
3 one
4 two
5 three
6 >> temp'
7 ans =
8 ott
9 nwh
10 eor
11   e
12   e
```

Hopefully, you noticed some of the issues with using character matrices. Let's try making cell variables instead, separating the elements with commas.

```
1 >> temp = { 'one', 'two' }
2 temp =
3      'one'    'two'
4 >> temp'
5 ans =
6      'one'
7      'two'
8 >> temp = { 'one', 'two', 'three' }
9 temp =
10     'one'    'two'    'three'
11 >> temp(1)
12 ans =
13     'one'
14 >> temp(3)
15 ans =
16     'three'
17 >> temp = { 'one'; 'two'; 'three' }
18 temp =
19     'one'
20     'two'
21     'three'
```

The key advantage of using cells is that you can easily store multiple strings, such as lists of words, in a single variable (as we did in the previous section with the word database).

2.7.1 Opening Your Own Data Files

While I can readily explain to you how to load the sample data that came with this book into MATLAB, that's not really why you are here. You are here to learn to use MATLAB to conduct your own analyses. However, unlike with the data provided here, I cannot anticipate how the data in your own research may be formatted. If you constructed your own data files to only consist of numbers, you can simply use `load` to import your data into MATLAB. This is what I personally do.

★ **TIP #16**

If you're feeling a bit adventurous, you can open files in a similar way to `load` using an approach similar to what we learned with `textscan`. Here you would again open and close the file with `fopen` and `fclose`, respectively. Here you would use `fscanf` instead of `textscan`. Once you are more comfortable with MATLAB, you may want to look into these functions further. ∎

It is also possible to read in data from Microsoft Excel (`.xls`) files directly into MATLAB with `xlsread`; however, this performs inconsistently across operating systems and depending on if Excel is installed on your machine. Due to these inconsistencies, we will not discuss `xlsread` here, but feel free to look into it yourself.

2.8 Making a New Directory

Since you're saving data and outputting data from MATLAB, you need to know where it's going! We already learned to navigate directories in Section 2.4.1; however, you don't know how to make directories yet. While you could just make them outside of MATLAB, if you need to make directories as part of your analysis (which you can later automate), making the directories through MATLAB can be essential. To make directories, we use `mkdir` (makes sense, no?).

```
1 >> pwd
2 ans =
3 /Users/chris/Desktop/matlabintro
4 >> mkdir('test')
5 >> cd('test')
6 >> pwd
7 ans =
8 /Users/chris/Desktop/matlabintro/test
```

2.9 Getting Data Out of MATLAB

Being able to analyze data is great. But sometimes you need to *store* your data matrix for later or to get it out of MATLAB completely. Having code to do the analysis that you can copy and paste is important, but you don't want to reanalyze the same data set every time (and we will learn to make our own analysis functions later too!).

For now, we're going to go back to the `iqbrain` data set, as it's a bit more straightforward to work with. If you don't have it loaded anymore, let's clear our workspace, go back, and get that data into MATLAB again.

```
1 >> cd('..')
2 >> cd('iqbrain')
3 >> clear,clc
4 >> iqbrain = load('data.txt');
```

Before you try any of the methods to save data, we probably should now go back to our test directory, so we don't accidentally overwrite our original data files. (This is also very important to keep in mind in the future!)

2.9.1 Using save

You can use the `save` function to save all of the variables in your MATLAB workspace.

```
1 >> save('everything')
```

You can also specify which variables you want to save, rather than just saving all of them. To do this, list the names of the variables you want to save in single quotes (so that the names are strings).

```
1 >> save('data','iqbrain')
```

> ★ TIP #17
>
> If we had more variables in our workspace, we could also use wildcards (i.e., "*") to save multiple variables that all start with the same first few characters, without listing them all directly. ∎

2.9.2 Using `dlmwrite`

Another way to save data that is readily readable in most other programs is to use `dlmwrite`. This function works similarly to `dlmread` but instead outputs the data.

```
1 >> dlmwrite('data.txt',iqbrain)
```

With its default settings, `dlmwrite` will separate the data from each column with a comma. This is commonly referred to as "CSV," which is an abbreviation for "comma separated values." Below are the first few lines of the text file:

```
1 2,133,118,64.5,8.1693e+05
2 1,140,NaN,72.5,1.0011e+06
3 1,139,143,73.3,1.0384e+06
4 1,133,172,68.8,9.6535e+05
5 2,137,147,65,9.5154e+05
```

That mostly worked, but it looks like the column with the brain size got converted into scientific notation. We can solve this by telling MATLAB to use the %f formatting.

```
1 >> dlmwrite('data.txt',iqbrain,'precision','%f'
```

Now, we look at the first few lines, and it's a bit better.

```
1 2.000000,133.000000,118.000000,64.500000,816932.000000
2 1.000000,140.000000,NaN,72.500000,1001121.000000
3 1.000000,139.000000,143.000000,73.300000,1038437.000000
4 1.000000,133.000000,172.000000,68.800000,965353.000000
5 2.000000,137.000000,147.000000,65.000000,951545.000000
```

Well, we aren't in scientific notation, but we really don't need all of those decimal places. We can solve this by telling MATLAB to not have any decimal places.

```
1 >> dlmwrite('data.txt',iqbrain,'precision','%.0f'
```

Let's take a look at the first few lines.

```
1 2,133,118,64,816932
2 1,140,NaN,72,1001121
3 1,139,143,73,1038437
4 1,133,172,69,965353
5 2,137,147,65,951545
```

That's better!

As with `dlmread`, we can specify how data in different columns are delimited.

```
1 >> dlmwrite('data.txt',iqbrain,'precision','%.0f','delimiter','\t')
```

As expected, the data from each column are now separated by a tab:

```
1 2    133 118 64    816932
2 1    140 NaN 72    1001121
3 1    139 143 73    1038437
4 1    133 172 69    965353
5 2    137 147 65    951545
```

2.9.3 More Control in Outputting Your Data

To give you a bit more control when exporting your data, I have also written an additional function called `imbmatlab2txt`. This function will not only write the data stored in a variable to a text file (".txt") but will also allow you to specify headers for each column. To specify the headers, we will use our newly learned type of variable, "cell arrays." With respect to `imbmatlab2txt`, you need to specify the headers with single quotes around each column's header, with the list of column headers as a cell array. The function can be used in the following way: `imbmatlab2txt(filename, data, headers)`.

```
1 >> headers = {'Gender', 'IQ', 'Weight', 'Height', 'BrainSize'};
2 >> imbmatlab2txt('data.txt',iqbrain,headers)
3 Data written to data.txt.
```

Let's take a look at the first few lines of our newly written text file.

```
1 Gender    IQ    Weight   Height    BrainSize
2 2     133   118   64    816932
3 1     140   NaN   72    1001121
4 1     139   143   73    1038437
5 1     133   172   69    965353
```

Great, we have headers in the outputted file now! Now, let's practice this a bit more with a few exercises and then move on to some basic analyses.

EXERCISES

Starting from the `matlabintro` folder, try the following exercises.

1. Make a directory called "`ch2test`."

2. Switch into your new directory, list its contents, and then go back up to the previous directory.

3. Store the path to the current directory in a string.

4. Try and read in the `iqbrain` data, without referring back to the chapter too much.

5. Try and read in the `worddb` data.

See page 193 for the solutions. In this chapter, we mainly learned how to better interact with MATLAB, so there isn't too much to try exercises with. Don't worry, we will learn to do some basic analyses in the next chapter!

FUNCTION REVIEW

Directories: `pwd dir ls cd mkdir`

Loading: `load dlmread textscan fopen fclose xlsread`

General: `repmat { }`

Saving: `save dlmwrite`

3

BASIC ANALYSES

If you were starting to get impatient about when we will actually start to analyze some data, the wait is over! By this point we can now manually enter data, navigate through folders on our computer (via MATLAB), and load and save data files. Now comes the good part!

Before we begin, we should get you acquainted with the single function that you will use the most often.

3.1 Don't Be Afraid to Ask for Help!

MATLAB has a great built-in help function that displays information about a function in the main command window (`help`). `help` displays the syntax required to use the function, as well as listing some related functions. If you're not sure what the function you're looking for is called, and guessing doesn't seem to work, MATLAB also has a function called `lookfor`. Using `lookfor`, we just tell MATLAB what we are trying to do (in the form of keywords), and MATLAB searches the descriptions of all of the functions and tells us where our keyword comes up.

For example, if you want to find the average of a list of values, you might think that you just need to use a function called "average," right? If you were in Microsoft Excel, you would be correct. However, this is not Excel. In MATLAB (and in statistics!), we use the function called "mean." If you didn't know this yet, this would be a great opportunity to try `lookfor`. Even though you know now, I suggest you try `lookfor` and `help` anyway.

```
1 >> lookfor average
2 MEAN    Average or mean value.
3 >> help  mean
4  MEAN     Average or mean value.
5    For vectors,  MEAN(X)  is the mean value of the elements in X. For
6    matrices, MEAN(X) is a row vector containing the mean value of
7    each column. For N-D arrays, MEAN(X) is the mean value of the
8    elements along the first non-singleton dimension of X.
9
10    MEAN(X,DIM) takes the mean along the dimension DIM of X.
11
12    Example: If X = [0 1 2
13                     3 4 5]
14
15    then mean(X,1) is [1.5 2.5 3.5] and mean(X,2) is [1
16                                                       4]
17
18    See also median, std, min, max, var, cov, mode.
19
20    Reference page in Help browser
21       doc mean
```

A second, more detailed help command also exists, called doc. Using the doc function opens a separate help window and looks up the function in question. The doc function differs from help in that it provides a more detailed description of the function, as well as more examples of how to use the function. doc also may include tables and figures in its examples, rather than just text.

```
1 >> doc mean
```

★ **TIP #18**

Don't underestimate the usefulness of help and doc when you aren't sure what function to use. Though they may be cryptic at times, they often can give you some direction as to how to solve your problem! ∎

3.2 Descriptive Statistics

Now, we'll need to start doing some simple analyses. Usually some things we need to do are average values across, find the median, find standard deviations, and find out how many values we have.

- `mean`: calculates the average/mean of the given numbers.
- `median`: calculates the median from a data set.
- `std`: calculates the standard deviation.
- `var`: calculates the variance.
- `min`: reports the smallest value in the specified data set.
- `max`: reports the largest value in the specified data set.
- `sum`: sums up all of the values in the data set.
- `length`: calculates how "large" a matrix is (only outputs the largest dimension of the matrix).
- `size`: gets the lengths of *all* dimensions of a matrix.
- `sort`: rearranges the rows to be "sort"-ed by their value.

Of course, you would need to also include the variable you want to do the operation on. For example, the mean of matrix M would be `mean(M)`.

For now, let's revisit our `iqbrain` data set.

```
1 >> iqbrain = load('data.txt');
```

Let's try our new functions to check out the size of our iqbrain matrix.

```
1 >> length(iqbrain)
2 ans =
3      40
4 >> size(iqbrain)
5 ans =
6      40     5
```

To calculate the average IQ for the participants in this study, we simply ask MATLAB using the `mean`.

```
1 >> mean(iqbrain)
2 ans =
3    1.0e+05 *
4      0.0000    0.0011      NaN      NaN    9.0876
```

Hmm ... that doesn't quite work. If we use the `mean` function, it calculates the mean for each column. However, the IQs are only in one of our columns. If you recall from Chapter 1, we learned how to select only portions of our data, which is our second column. For your reference, I'll also show you how to select the fifth row (here, participant), rather than column.

```
1 >> iqbrain(:,2)
2 ans =
3     133
4     140
5     139
6     133
7     137
8     ...
9 >> iqbrain(5,:)
10 ans =
11              2         137         147          65       951545
```

Now, for the mean . . .

```
1 >> mean(iqbrain(:,2))
2 ans =
3    113.4500
```

★ TIP #19

Never name a variable with the same name as a function! For example, mean = mean(iqbrain). While this command will work, from this point on mean will refer to your new variable rather than the MATLAB function. If you do make this mistake, using clear to clear the variable from your workspace should get you back on track! To do this, type clear('mean'). ∎

Similarly, we can also calculate the minimum, maximum, and standard deviation.

```
1 >> min(iqbrain(:,2))
2 ans =
3      77
4 >> max(iqbrain(:,2))
5 ans =
6     144
7 >> std(iqbrain(:,2))
8 ans =
9    24.0821
```

> ★ TIP #20
>
> When using some of these functions, primarily `mean` and `std`, you may realize MATLAB is doing the analysis along a dimension other than the one you want. In these cases, you want to specify what dimension for MATLAB to do the function on. However, the developers of MATLAB decided not to make both functions work quite the same way. If you want to do the mean across the second dimension (across columns) you would do `mean([variable name],2)`. However, the respective standard deviation would be `std([variable name],[],2)`. This is because `std` takes a different variable in the second position, rather than the dimension to do the calculation across. A dimension can also be specified in the `size` function, simply as `size([variable name],[dimension number])`. ■

3.3 Comparing Values

Next, we need to be able to compare some numbers. The main relational operators in MATLAB are as follows:

`=`	sets values[†]
`~`	not
`==`	is equal to
`~=`	is not equal to
`<`	is lesser than
`>`	is greater than
`=<`	is less than or equal to
`=>`	is greater than or equal to

When we give MATLAB two values, with one of these operators in the middle, it tells us if that statement is true or not! MATLAB tells us this by responding with either 1 (true) or 0 (false). This kind of response is called "Boolean" logic.

[†] a single equal sign alone does *not* compare values, but was still included here for completion, and to remind you of this fact.

```
 1 >> 1 == 1
 2 ans =
 3       1
 4 >> 1 == 0
 5 ans =
 6       0
 7 >> 42 > 10
 8 ans =
 9       1
10 >> iqbrain(:,2)' > 100
11 ans =
12   Columns 1 through 10
13          1      1      1    1    1    0    1    0    0    1
14   Columns 11 through 20
15          1      1      1    1    0    0    1    0    1    0
16   Columns 21 through 30
17          0      0      1    1    0    1    0    1    0    1
18   Columns 31 through 40
19          1      1      1    0    0    1    1    0    0    0
```

Soon you will learn to

- Select specific subsets of data based on logical statements (p. 53)
- Calculate descriptive statistics for experimental conditions (p. 45)

3.4 Working With Logical Operators

Okay, so you can compare numbers and see if they're greater than, lesser than, or equal to each other. We can also see where one number is not the same as another set. Let's not stop there though! To do more complicated comparisons we can use and and or operations as well.

While combinations of these operators may seem trivial, or even irrelevant, they will lay the foundation of your data analysis. As such, I will explain their use through several different approaches.

First, consider that we have one data set of values, called "A," as well as a second data set, labeled "B." If we are only interested in A, then we can stop there (Figure 3.1a).

```
1 >> A = [ 1 1 1 1 0 0 0 0 ];
2 >> B = [ 1 0 1 0 1 0 1 0 ];
3 >> Aonly = A
4 Aonly =
5      1   1   1   1   0   0   0   0
```

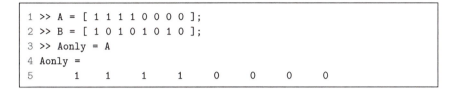

Figure 3.1 Venn diagrams of Boolean operators.

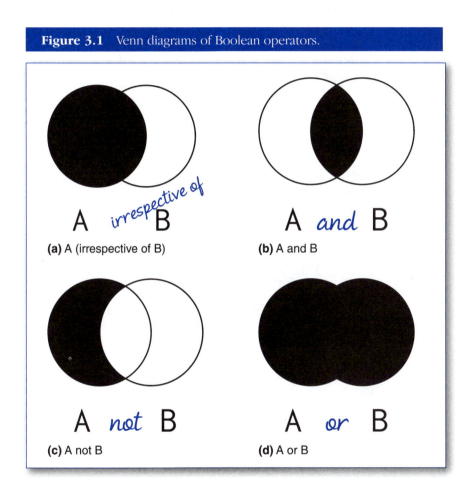

(a) A (irrespective of B)

(b) A and B

(c) A not B

(d) A or B

If we are interested in values that are present in both A *and* B, then we use *and* (Figure 3.1b). In MATLAB, *and* is represented by an & (ampersand) symbol.

```
1 >> AandB = A & B
2 AandB =
3     1    0    1    0    0    0    0    0
```

If we only want to consider cases where values are present in A, but *not* in B, we use the Boolean operator *not* (Figure 3.1c). In MATLAB, *not* is represented by a ~ (tilde) symbol.

```
1 >> AnotB = A & ~B
2 AnotB =
3     0    1    0    1    0    0    0    0
```

Last, if we are satisfied if any value is a part of either A *or* B, then *or* is the appropriate operator (Figure 3.1d). In MATLAB, *or* is represented by a | (bar or pipe) symbol.

```
1 >> AorB = A | B
2 AorB =
3     1    1    1    1    1    0    1    0
```

Of potentially similar usefulness is when A is not equal to B, which would include both "sides" of the Venn diagram, without the middle. Knowing the above operators, this could be achieved in several ways:

```
1 >> A ~= B
2 ans =
3     0    1    0    1    1    0    1    0
4 >> AorB - AandB
5 ans =
6     0    1    0    1    1    0    1    0
7 >> (A & ~B) | (~ A & B)
8 ans =
9     0    1    0    1    1    0    1    0
```

Okay, admittedly, that was a bit abstract. Let's try using our `iqbrain` data set to make this a bit more relevant.

First, let's calculate the mean IQ for all the participants in our sample again.

```
1 >> mean(iqbrain(:,2))
2 ans =
3    113.4500
```

If you print out the contents of `iqbrain`, you can see that there are many participants with IQs lower than 100. Can you check how many? What proportion of the sample had IQs less than 100?

```
1 >> nLowIQ = sum(iqbrain(:,2)' < 100)
2 nLowIQ =
3      16
4 >> pLowIQ = sum(iqbrain(:,2)' < 100) ./ length(iqbrain)
5 pLowIQ =
6      0.4000
```

See, now that we've learned the basics, it's fairly easy to start working with data! Let's try a few more:

What were the highest and lowest IQs in the sample?

```
1 >> lowIQ = min(iqbrain(:,2))
2 lowIQ =
3      77
4 >> highIQ = max(iqbrain(:,2))
5 highIQ =
6    144
```

3.5 Isolating Specific Portions of Data

Now, we have descriptive statistics and the ability to combine different types of data with Boolean operators. However, one important thing we cannot do yet is look up specific values across conditions.

In addition to having MATLAB report 1s and 0s, it would be more useful to obtain the index values when the statement is true. This can be done with the `find` function.

```
1 >> find(A)
2 ans =
3      1    2    3    4
4 >> find(B)
5 ans =
6      1    3    5    7
```

This can also be applied to the use of the Boolean statements from the previous section.

```
1 >> find(A & B)
2 ans =
3     1     3
4 >> find(AandB)
5 ans =
6     1     3
```

Additionally, MATLAB also has the function `intersect`, which is specifically made to output values that are part of two sets of values.

```
1 >> intersect(find(A),find(B))
2 ans =
3     1     3
```

We can also apply this logic to *not* statements and use the MATLAB function `setdiff` to obtain a list of values that are part of one set but not another (unidirectionally, as in Figure 3.1c).

```
1 >> find(AnotB)
2 ans =
3     2     4
4 >> setdiff(find(A),find(B))
5 ans =
6     2     4
7 >> setdiff(find(B),find(A))
8 ans =
9     5     7
```

While not terribly useful on its own, with the use of these indices and multiple data sets that are organized through similar ways, we can find when both things are true. For example, what if I asked you *which* participants were male? (Reminder: **Gender=1** corresponds to males.)

```
1 >> find(iqbrain(:,1)==1)
2 ans =
3      2
4      3
5      4
6      9
7     10
8     ...
```

What about which participants had IQs above 100?

```
1 >> find(iqbrain(:,2)>100)
2 ans =
3     1
4     2
5     3
6     4
7     5
8    ...
```

Let's try and put those both together: Which participants were males with IQs above 100?

```
1 >> find(iqbrain(:,1)==1 & iqbrain(:,2)>100)
2 ans =
3      2
4      3
5      4
6     10
7     12
8     13
9     24
10     26
11     28
12     32
13     33
14     37
```

How many participants is that? What about how many participants were females with IQs above 100?

```
1 >> nMaleHighIQ = length(find(iqbrain(:,1)==1 & iqbrain(:,2)>100))
2 nMaleHighIQ =
3     12
4 >> nFemaleHighIQ = length(find(iqbrain(:,1)==2 & iqbrain(:,2)>100))
5 nFemaleHighIQ =
6     11
```

3.6 Simple Analyses Involving Text Data

Hopefully, you are starting to see why this type of code can be so important to our analyses. Let's try this type of analysis out with the word database example data set. First, let's load the data in again.

```
1 >> clear,clc
2 >> fid = fopen('JanschewitzB386appB.txt','r');
3 >> formatstring = [ '%s %s' repmat(' %f' ,1,19)  ];
4 >> worddata=textscan(fid,formatstring,'headerlines',5, ...
5 'delimiter','\t');
6 >> fclose(fid);
```

★ TIP #21

Variable names in MATLAB *cannot* start with a number. For example, naming a variable as 460 words would produce an error. Give it a try and see for yourself! ∎

As a reminder, the headers for the columns are listed below and also in the `data_legend.txt` file in the same folder as the data.

```
 1 Word
 2 Type
 3 Letters
 4 Syllables
 5 K&F - Freq.
 6 ANEW - Valence
 7 ANEW - Arousal
 8 Personal Use - Mean
 9 Personal Use - SD
10 Familiarity - Mean
11 Familiarity - SD
12 Offensiveness - Mean
13 Offensiveness - SD
14 Tabooness - Mean
15 Tabooness - SD
16 Valence - Mean
17 Valence - SD
18 Arousal - Mean
19 Arousal - SD
20 Imageability - Mean
21 Imageability - SD
```

Let's try and get the mean arousal ratings for the taboo words. First, we need to use `find` to get their row numbers within the database. Remember that we ended up with a cell array when we first learned to load this data using `textscan` (p. 32).

```
1 >> find(worddata{2}=='taboo')
2 ??? Undefined function or method 'eq' for input arguments
3 of type 'cell'.
```

Unfortunately, you can't use the simple comparison operators with text. That being said, it kind of makes sense that strings need to work a bit differently since "greater than" and "less than" don't really make sense with strings. To do comparisons with strings, we get to use another MATLAB function: **strcmp**.

```
 1 >> strcmp(worddata{2},{'taboo'})
 2 ans =
 3       1
 4       1
 5       1
 6       1
 7       1
 8       ...
 9 >> find(strcmp(worddata{2},{'taboo'}))
10 ans =
11       1
12       2
13       3
14       4
15       5
16       ...
```

Okay, now we can look up the arousal ratings for only these words, which is simply this selection of rows.

```
1 >> worddata{18}(find(strcmp(worddata{2},{'taboo'})))
2 ans =
3       4.0100
4       4.0800
5       4.7400
6       3.1800
7       4.6200
8       ...
```

And now we just get the mean of these values! Let's also try the mean imageability and tabooness.

```
1 >> mAroTaboo = mean(worddata{18}(find(strcmp(worddata{2}, ...
2 {'taboo'}))))
3 mAroTaboo =
4     4.3357
5 >> mImagTaboo = mean(worddata{20}(find(strcmp(worddata{2}, ...
6 {'taboo'}))))
7 mImagTaboo =
8     4.5410
9 >> mTabTaboo = mean(worddata{14}(find(strcmp(worddata{2}, ...
10 {'taboo'}))))
11 mTabTaboo =
12     4.8284
```

If you are having a bit of trouble following the code above, don't worry; we'll discuss the combining of multiple functions more in the next section.

Given this data set, one more particularly useful analysis would be to make a list of our word types. This can easily be done by passing the column of word types into a new function: unique. This function is great for isolating only the *unique* values within a column of values. It automatically sorts the values, rather than listing them in their order of occurrence.

```
1 >> unique(worddata{2})
2 ans =
3     ' '
4     'neg hi ar'
5     'neg lo ar'
6     'pos hi ar'
7     'pos lo ar'
8     'rel neu'
9     'taboo'
10    'unrel neu'
```

This almost works, but it seems we also have an empty entry. This is a remnant of the extra comment lines we noted at the bottom of the file earlier. We can solve this simply by constraining our data that goes into the unique function to only the rows with the actual words.

```
1 >> types=unique(worddata{2}(1:460))
2 types =
3     'neg hi ar'
4     'neg lo ar'
5     'pos hi ar'
6     'pos lo ar'
7     'rel neu'
8     'taboo'
9     'unrel neu'
```

Now, we can also get the means for other word types relatively easily.

```
1 >> mAroNegHi=mean(worddata{18}(find(strcmp(worddata{2},types{1}))))
2 mAroNegHi =
3     3.1987
4 >> mAroNegLo=mean(worddata{18}(find(strcmp(worddata{2},types{2}))))
5 mAroNegLo =
6     2.5715
```

★ TIP #22

If `strcmp` is useful for your work, you may also want to look into `strncmp`. ■

3.7 Combining Functions

Now, you can compare data in lots of ways! However, to conduct the more "interesting" analyses, you often have to string together several MATLAB functions into one coherent line of code. To do this, you need to start from the basics and *work outward* to get to the end result.

To some, this may seem like common sense (if you understand what I mean by working outward), but for some, this is a real leap of logic, so try and bear with me. When you want to do a particular analysis, you need to decompose it into manageable steps. Then, you need to begin from the most basic, initial step and build up. However, to do this you need to work outward. Let's try an example:

In the previous section, I came up with the following line as the code to calculate the mean arousal for only the taboo words.

```
1 >> mAroTaboo = mean(worddata{18}(find(strcmp(worddata{2},{'taboo'}))))
2 mAroTaboo =
3     4.3357
```

Let's start from the beginning and work out how I came to this. First, we begin with our columns for the word types and the mean arousal ratings.

```
 1 >> worddata{2}
 2 ans =
 3      'taboo'
 4      'taboo'
 5      'taboo'
 6      'taboo'
 7      'taboo'
 8      ...
 9 >> worddata{18}
10 ans =
11      4.0100
12      4.0800
13      4.7400
14      3.1800
15      4.6200
16      ...
```

Using the operators we learned for comparing values, let's ask MATLAB to show us when the word is of the 'taboo' type.

```
1 >> strcmp(worddata{2},{'taboo'})
2 ans =
3      1
4      1
5      1
6      1
7      1
8      ...
```

Now, we will ask MATLAB to find the indices where this comparison was reported to be "true" (i.e., 1).

```
1 >> find(strcmp(worddata{2},{'taboo'}))
2 ans =
3      1
4      2
5      3
6      4
7      5
8      ...
```

Next, we need to ask MATLAB to show us the arousal ratings, but only for these selected rows.

```
1 >> worddata{18}(find(strcmp(worddata{2},{'taboo'})))
2 ans =
3      4.0100
4      4.0800
5      4.7400
6      3.1800
7      4.6200
8      . . .
```

We're almost there! Let's ask MATLAB to calculate the mean of these values.

```
1 >> mean(worddata{18}(find(strcmp(worddata{2},{'taboo'}))))
2 ans =
3      4.3357
```

And now we arrive at the same line of code and output value as we began. Hopefully that made sense. Before we move on, let's try replicating this logic with another analysis—this time using the iqbrain data set.

```
1 >> clear,clc
2 >> iqbrain = load('data.txt');
```

In this sample, what was the mean IQ for (a) males and (b) females? Which was higher?

The first answer, the mean IQ for males, can be calculated using the line below.

```
1 >> mMaleIQ = mean(iqbrain(find(iqbrain(:,1)==1),2))
2 mMaleIQ =
3    115
```

Give it a try and see if you can replicate it yourself or at least understand parts of it.

How'd you do? Hopefully, you understood most of it. Regardless, let's try and work through the steps incrementally that led us to that "final" line of code. First, let's take a look at the data stored in the iqbrain variable.

```
1 >> iqbrain
2 iqbrain =
3    1.0e+06 *
4      0.0000    0.0001    0.0001    0.0001    0.8169
5      0.0000    0.0001       NaN    0.0001    1.0011
6      0.0000    0.0001    0.0001    0.0001    1.0384
7      0.0000    0.0001    0.0002    0.0001    0.9654
8      0.0000    0.0001    0.0001    0.0001    0.9515
9      ...
```

Notice that it's all in scientific notation, making it a bit harder to read. Let's look at only the first four columns, without showing the brain-size column.

```
1 >> iqbrain(:,1:4)
2 ans =
3      2.0000    133.0000    118.0000    64.5000
4      1.0000    140.0000         NaN    72.5000
5      1.0000    139.0000    143.0000    73.3000
6      1.0000    133.0000    172.0000    68.8000
7      2.0000    137.0000    147.0000    65.0000
8      ...
```

Okay, so let's focus on just the column that denotes the gender.

```
1 >> iqbrain(:,1)
2 ans =
3      2
4      1
5      1
6      1
7      2
8      ...
```

Okay, now we check when the gender column matches the value for males.

```
1 >> iqbrain(:,1)==1
2 ans =
3      0
4      1
5      1
6      1
7      0
8      ...
```

Next, we get the corresponding participant/row numbers.

```
 1 >> find(iqbrain(:,1)==1)
 2 ans =
 3      2
 4      3
 5      4
 6      9
 7     10
 8    ...
```

Now, get the IQs again, and then the IQs for these specific row numbers.

```
 1 >> iqbrain(:,2)
 2 ans =
 3      133
 4      140
 5      139
 6      133
 7      137
 8      ...
 9 >> iqbrain(find(iqbrain(:,1)==1),2)
10 ans =
11      140
12      139
13      133
14       89
15      133
16      ...
```

We're almost there! Now, we just need to calculate the mean for this set of IQs.

```
1 >> mMaleIQ = mean(iqbrain(find(iqbrain(:,1)==1),2))
2 mMaleIQ =
3    115
```

At this point, it should be almost trivial to get the mean IQ for the females.

```
1 >> mFemaleIQ = mean(iqbrain(find(iqbrain(:,1)==2),2))
2 mFemaleIQ =
3    111.9000
```

It looks like the IQs are slightly higher for the males in this sample. Right now, we can't say anything about this difference being statistically significant; that will come later.

Let's try one more analysis and learn something along the way:

In this sample, were IQs relatively higher for taller participants? What was the median height of the participants (in inches)? What was the mean IQ for participants taller or shorter than the median?

```
1 >> medHeight = median(iqbrain(:,4))
2 medHeight =
3    NaN
```

Hmm . . . I don't think that's what you were expecting. The problem is that in this column, as well as the height column, the researchers did not provide the height or weight of the participants for confidentiality reasons. But how do we do the descriptive statistics without these? MATLAB clearly doesn't know what to tell us.

3.8 What Is NaN?

Sometimes when we try analyzing our data, MATLAB will respond with 'NaN'. NaN stands for "Not a Number." Basically, MATLAB doesn't think it can answer your command with a number. You just encountered one such instance of this occurring. We can easily find these cases using `isnan`.

```
1 >> find(isnan(iqbrain(:,4)))
2 ans =
3    21
```

In this particular case, the researchers who conducted the `iqbrain` study did not provide the height and weight of a few participants when sharing the data set.

To calculate the median, ignoring the NaN values, we can use the `nanmedian` function rather than `median`.

```
1 >> medHeight = nanmedian(iqbrain(:,4))
2 medHeight =
3    68
```

For other descriptive statistics with NaNs, there also exist other comparable functions such as **nanmean** and **nanstd**. Unfortunately, these NaN-accomodating functions are not part of the core MATLAB distribution and are only included in the Statistics Toolbox. Simply, these functions skip over the NaN values and calculate the appropriate statistic.

If you need such a function but do not have the Statistics Toolbox, you can easily develop your own implementation using isnan. (Later, we'll make our own function equivalent to nanmedian, nanmean, etc.)

```
1 >> medHeight = median(iqbrain(~isnan(iqbrain(:,4)),4))
2 medHeight =
3     68
```

Now, to answer the actual question regarding IQ and height:

```
1 >> mean(iqbrain(find(iqbrain(:,4)>medHeight & ...
2 ~isnan(iqbrain(:,4))),2))
3 ans =
4    116.6316
5 >> mean(iqbrain(find(iqbrain(:,4)<medHeight & ...
6 ~ isnan(iqbrain(:,4))),2))
7 ans =
8    113.6471
```

It looks like the mean IQ is a bit higher for the taller participants.

3.9 Unbalanced or Unexpected Parenthesis or Bracket

One common error that is likely to arise now that we're making these more complicated lines of code is to accidentally not close all of our brackets or to open too many of them. When this occurs, MATLAB will report an error as below.

```
1 >> mean(iqbrain(find(iqbrain(:,4)<medHeight & ~isnan(iqbrain(:,4)),2))
2 ??? mean(iqbrain(find(iqbrain(:,4)<medHeight & ~isnan(iqbrain(:,4)),2))
3                                                                      |
4 Error: Expression or statement is incorrect-possibly unbalanced (,  {,
5 or [.
```

When you do come across this error, reread your code carefully and hopefully you'll spot the missing bracket. This would also be a good instance to break the line down and work outward again to rewrite the line of code in question.

EXERCISES

Let's take the training wheels off and try out some of the new functions and operations that we learned in this chapter!

1. How many females were in the `iqbrain` data set?

2. What was the average height of the participants? What were the heights of the tallest and shortest participants? (in inches)

3. What was the weight of the tallest participant? (in pounds)

4. In the `worddb` data set, what were the most positive (valence) words?

5. Which word rated highest on the personal-use scale? Is it the same as the most familiar word?

6. What is the average valence for each word type?

7. Are taboo words more imageable than high-arousal positive and negative words? Are high-arousal words more imageable than low-arousal words?

8. From this database, what are the 10 most imageable words? Which words rank 100 to 110 in terms of word length?

9. What is the median number of letters and syllables across all word types?

See page 194 for the solutions. Now we're making some good progress! Hopefully now you are starting to feel much more capable within MATLAB and can start conducting some basic analyses of your own data. In the next chapter, we will take this one step further and learn to plot our data.

FUNCTION REVIEW

Help: `help lookfor doc`

Basic analyses: `mean median std var min max sum length size sort`

Comparisons: `= ~ == ~= < > =< => strcmp intersect setdiff`

General: `unique`

NaN related: `isnan nanmean nanmedian nanstd`

4

MAKING FIGURES

Now that we can organize our data and perform some simple analyses, we need to be able to view our data as a figure. Sometimes, it's hard to see patterns in your data until you first plot them, but you will also learn how to make publication-ready figures.

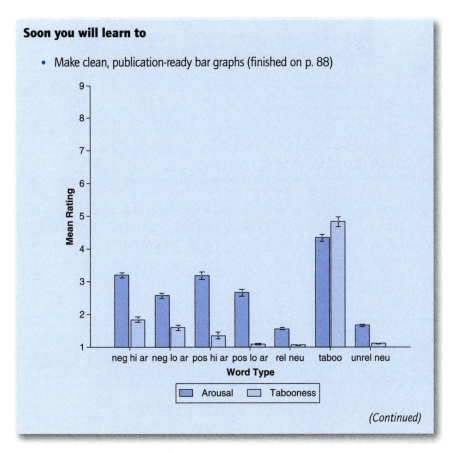

Soon you will learn to

- Make clean, publication-ready bar graphs (finished on p. 88)

(Continued)

(Continued)

- Calculate inferential statistics such as *t* tests and correlation coefficients (pp. 156 and 165)
- Create more complicated figures, such as a heat map of eye fixations from an eye-tracking study (p. 182)

Source: Cerf et al. (2007).

4.1 Plotting Fundamentals: Step by Step

First, we need to start from the basics: Making a bar graph, adding axes labels, and saving the figure so that it can be viewed outside of MATLAB. For now, let's use the word database data set and make bars for the arousal ratings of each of the seven word types.

```
1 >> fid = fopen('JanschewitzB386appB.txt','r');
2 >> formatstring = [ '%s %s' repmat(' %f ' ,1,19) ];
3 >> worddata=textscan(fid,formatstring,'headerlines',5, ...
4 'delimiter','\t');
5 >> fclose(fid);
```

First, we need to get the means for each word type.

```
 1 >> types=unique(worddata{2}(1:460))
 2 types =
 3      'neg hi ar'
 4      'neg lo ar'
 5      'pos hi ar'
 6      'pos lo ar'
 7      'rel neu'
 8      'taboo'
 9      'unrel neu'
10 >> i=1;
11 >> mAro(i)=mean(worddata{18}(find(strcmp(worddata{2},types{i}))));
12 >> i=i+1;
13 >> mAro(i)=mean(worddata{18}(find(strcmp(worddata{2},types{i}))));
14 >> i=i+1;
15 >> mAro(i)=mean(worddata{18}(find(strcmp(worddata{2},types{i}))));
16 >> i=i+1;
17 >> mAro(i)=mean(worddata{18}(find(strcmp(worddata{2},types{i}))));
18 >> i=i+1;
19 >> mAro(i)=mean(worddata{18}(find(strcmp(worddata{2},types{i}))));
20 >> i=i+1;
21 >> mAro(i)=mean(worddata{18}(find(strcmp(worddata{2},types{i}))));
22 >> i=i+1;
23 >> mAro(i)=mean(worddata{18}(find(strcmp(worddata{2},types{i}))));
24 >> mAro
25 mAro =
26      3.1987    2.5715    3.1730    2.6630    1.5595    4.3357    1.6551
```

(*Note*: Later, we'll learn how to do that without the repetitive lines of code.)

Drawing a bar graph from this is simple, we need to feed this data into the MATLAB function `bar`.

```
1 >> bar(mAro)
```

Your resulting figure should look like Figure 4.1.

Okay, that works to some degree, for just viewing the data ourselves. However, if we want to show this to anyone else (e.g., a collaborator, your supervisor, a lab/office mate), we should probably add in some more details. For starters, let's add some axes labels (`xlabel`, `ylabel`) and a title (`title`).

```
1 >> xlabel('Word Type')
2 >> ylabel('Mean Rating')
3 >> title('Arousal')
```

Figure 4.1   First plot of mean arousal ratings for each word type.

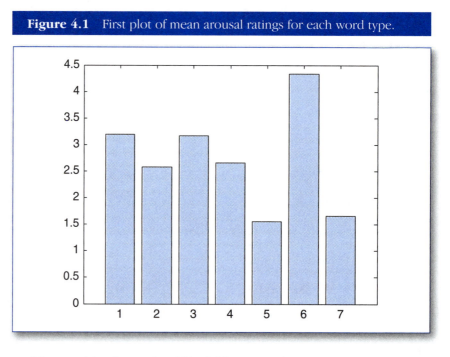

Your resulting figure should look like Figure 4.2.

Figure 4.2   Plot of mean arousal ratings, now with labels.

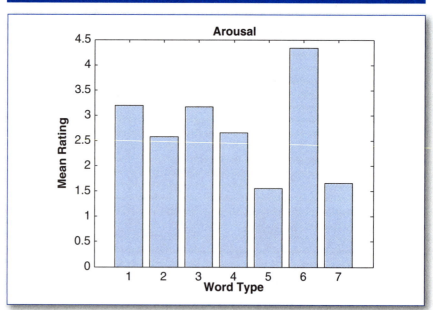

Okay, that's a bit better! But now that we have the axes labeled, it's clear that we need to adjust things a bit. The ratings can range from 1 to 9; participants can't give words a rating of 0, so it doesn't make sense to include values less than 1. To adjust the boundaries of the figure, we need to use the `axis` function. Here we specify four values, the lower and upper bounds to use for the *x*-axis, followed by the lower and upper bounds for the *y*-axis. Let's use 0 to 8 for the *x*-axis and 1 to 9 for the *y*-axis.

```
1 >> axis([0 8 1 9])
```

The next important thing is to set the positions of the *x*- and *y*-axis tick marks. We also need to replace the *x* ticks with actual labels instead of the numbers 1 to 7, which are relatively meaningless.

MATLAB automatically sets the *x*- and *y*-axis ticks for us, and here they increment by 1 in both cases. That works great for us, but if you adjust the size of the figure window, this can change. It would be better to make sure MATLAB keeps these settings for us. This change is a bit more complicated: MATLAB stores many axes-related properties in a special type of "object." We can access this information using a function called `get`. If we want to get properties from the current axes, we need to specify "`gca`," which stands for "get current axes." Right now we want to get the tick positions for the *x*-axis.

```
1 >> get(gca,'XTick')
2 ans =
3      1    2    3    4    5    6    7
```

If we want to change the information stored here, we can use the function `set`. If you're still a bit confused by `gca`, don't worry, we'll discuss it more extensively in Section 4.7.

```
1 >> set(gca,'XTick',1:7)
2 >> set(gca,'YTick',1:9)
```

Additionally, if we want to use text labels, we need a simple cell array composed of strings to 'replace' the numbers at each tick mark. If we wanted to use numbers, we could use a matrix of numbers instead. In our current situation, the `types` variable we made earlier is perfect.

```
1 >> set(gca,'XTickLabel',types)
```

You can see the updated figure with adjusted axis boundaries, tick positions, and labelling in Figure 4.3.

Figure 4.3 Plot of mean arousal ratings, now with more figure customization.

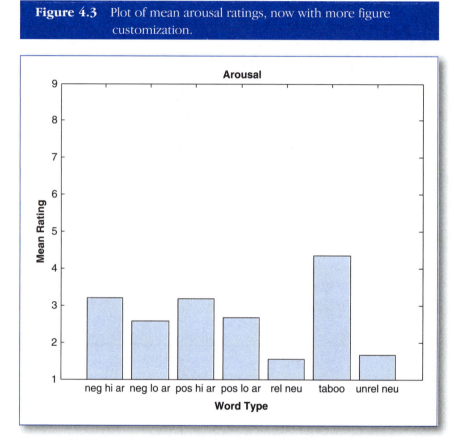

Now we have a figure that we can show to a colleague, but it still could use some work.

★ **TIP #23**

To get a full list of modifiable figure properties, type get(gca). ∎

4.2 Saving Your Figure

Before we move on to more complicated plotting techniques, we should probably know how to save figures. After all, your colleagues or supervisor can't always be physically nearby, and we shouldn't have to take screenshots!

If we want to "print" the figure as a PDF, you can use `print`.

```
1 >> print('-dpdf','mAro.pdf')
```

Here 'dpdf' represents MATLAB's PDF printing driver. There are many other formats you can print your figures to, including JPG and TIFF. To get the details regarding the other possible print drivers, ask MATLAB for a list (`help print` or `doc print`). While this function works well when working in MATLAB via commands, some may not want to make it so easy to accidentally overwrite an existing figure. Another option when printing your figures is to use the "Save" or "Save As" option from the figure's window in the MATLAB GUI. This method will also give you an option to save your figure in a variety of formats.

> **★ TIP #24**
>
> When using the GUI to save figures, be sure that the file name and the file format match! If you save a figure in the ".fig" format, but name it as ".pdf", you will run into many headaches later on! ∎

Now, we can begin to visualize our data! It doesn't look particularly pretty, but it works. Before we get into how to make our figures more presentable, let's first look into the other types of figures we can make.

> **★ TIP #25**
>
> You can also adjust the orientation of your figure in the printed PDF file using `orient`. ∎

4.3 A Sampling of the Many Ways to Plot Your Results

MATLAB provides us with many ways to illustrate our data. Below are a few of the more prevalent types of figures.

4.3.1 Horizontal Bar Graph

We can also make bar graphs with horizontal bars using the `barh` function, though its usage is otherwise identical. It actually looks quite good for this data (see Figure 4.4).

```
1 >> barh(mAro)
2 >> ylabel('Word Type')
3 >> xlabel('Mean Rating')
4 >> axis([1 9 0 8])
5 >> set(gca,'YTickLabel',types)
6 >> title('Arousal')
```

★ TIP #26

You may also want to look into the histogram function (`hist`)! ■

Figure 4.4   Horizontal bar graph.

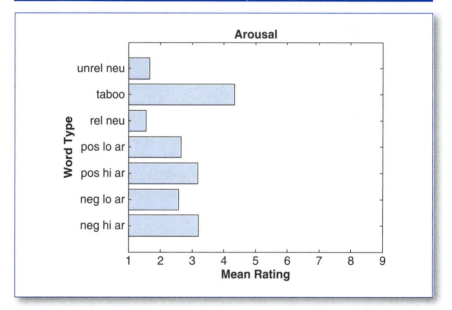

4.3.2 Line Graphs

Line graphs are another fairly important type of figure. For the most part, the `plot` works similar to the `bar` function. Let's make a line graph with the same data as the bar graph (Figure 4.5).

```
1 >> plot(mAro)
2 >> xlabel('Word Type')
3 >> ylabel('Mean Rating')
4 >> title('Arousal')
5 >> axis([0 8 1 9])
6 >> set(gca,'XTickLabel',types)
```

Figure 4.5   Line graph of mean arousal ratings for each word type.

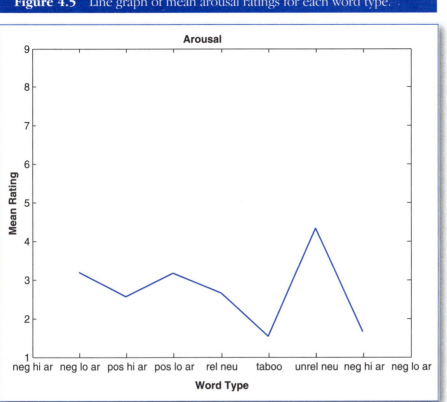

4.3.3 Error Bars

Before moving completely away from line graphs, let's try making a line graph *with* error bars. For researchers, this can be very important, as we often need to illustrate the robustness or consistency of our results through calculations of the standard error of the mean or with confidence intervals. To do this, we use a MATLAB function called `errorbar`, and along with the x and y values for the data, we also need to calculate the height of the error bar. Let's try and make a quick figure of the mean arousal ratings with the standard error of the mean (SEM) as our error bars (see Figure 4.6 on p. 77).

Before we can make the figure, we need to calculate the SEMs:

$$SEM(X, N) = std(X) / \sqrt{N}$$

`sqrt` is the MATLAB function for calculating the square root. However, this is also a bit more work as not all word types have the same number of words.

```
 1 >> i=1;
 2 >> stdAro(i)=std(worddata{18}(find(strcmp(worddata{2},types{i}))));
 3 >> nWord(i)=sum(strcmp(worddata{2},types{i}));
 4 >> i=i+1;
 5 >> stdAro(i)=std(worddata{18}(find(strcmp(worddata{2},types{i}))));
 6 >> nWord(i)=sum(strcmp(worddata{2},types{i}));
 7 >> i=i+1;
 8 >> stdAro(i)=std(worddata{18}(find(strcmp(worddata{2},types{i}))));
 9 >> nWord(i)=sum(strcmp(worddata{2},types{i}));
10 >> i=i+1;
11 >> stdAro(i)=std(worddata{18}(find(strcmp(worddata{2},types{i}))));
12 >> nWord(i)=sum(strcmp(worddata{2},types{i}));
13 >> i=i+1;
14 >> stdAro(i)=std(worddata{18}(find(strcmp(worddata{2},types{i}))));
15 >> nWord(i)=sum(strcmp(worddata{2},types{i}));
16 >> i=i+1;
17 >> stdAro(i)=std(worddata{18}(find(strcmp(worddata{2},types{i}))));
18 >> nWord(i)=sum(strcmp(worddata{2},types{i}));
19 >> i=i+1;
20 >> stdAro(i)=std(worddata{18}(find(strcmp(worddata{2},types{i}))));
21 >> nWord(i)=sum(strcmp(worddata{2},types{i}));
22 >> stdAro
23 stdAro =
24    0.5304    0.5505    0.8005    0.6961    0.2930    0.9896    0.3070
25 >> nWord
26 nWord =
27    46    46    46    46    92    92    92
28 >> semAro = stdAro./sqrt(nWord)
29 semAro =
30    0.0782    0.0812    0.1180    0.1026    0.0305    0.1032    0.0320
```

Try not to get too intimidated by the many lines of code here. Most of them are repetitive, and we will soon learn how to automate these types of analyses (p. 98).

Now, we can use the SEMs to make line graph with error bars!

```
1 >> errorbar(1:7,mAro,semAro)
2 >> xlabel('Word Type')
3 >> ylabel('Mean Rating')
4 >> title('Arousal')
5 >> axis([0 8 1 9])
6 >> set(gca,'XTickLabel',types)
```

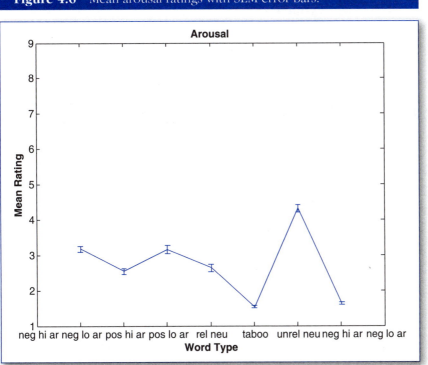

Figure 4.6   Mean arousal ratings with SEM error bars.

To make a bar graph with error bars, we will need to combine the `bar` and `errorbar` functions. Hold on until Section 4.5!

★ **TIP #27**

One other option with error bar figures is to have *asymmetric* error bars, such that the height of the upper and lower portions of the error bar are not equal. Use `help` to see if you can figure out how to do this. ∎

4.3.4 Scatterplots

Sometimes you may not want to connect your data points using lines or to collapse data into bars. When we want to visually inspect our data, we often want to use scatterplots. To make a scatterplot, we simply use the MATLAB function `scatter`.

Let's try making a scatterplot of the arousal and valence ratings, across all word types (Figure 4.7).

```
1 >> aro=worddata{18}(1:460);
2 >> val=worddata{16}(1:460);
3 >> scatter(val,aro)
4 >> xlabel('Valence')
5 >> ylabel('Arousal')
6 >> axis([1 9 1 9])
```

Figure 4.7   Scatterplot of arousal and valence ratings for all 460 words.

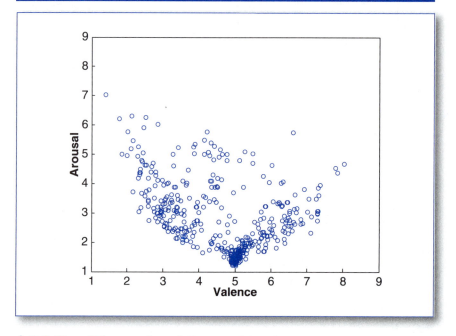

4.3.5 Two-Dimensional Image Matrices

Sometimes you want to look at data in an even more "raw" form, grids of squares, where each square represents a value from your matrix, color coded based on its value. These can be made using the **image** function. Correlation matrices are often made this way. The current data we have doesn't particularly lend itself to this type of a figure.

Usually in this type of figure, you would want to add a color bar using the **colorbar** function. This bar would denote the color-to-value mapping from the image matrix. Before we move on, you may want to try **imagesc**. In some cases, it may be better to maximize our ability to discriminate between values, rather than using a prespecified color mapping. **imagesc** takes the highest and lowest values present in the provided matrix of data and automatically sets those as the two most extreme colors.

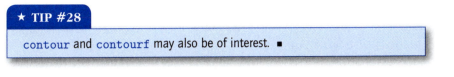

★ **TIP #28**

`contour` and `contourf` may also be of interest. ■

4.3.6 Pie Graphs

Though pie graphs may not be as common, they are nonetheless a notable type of figure. You can easily make them in MATLAB using the function `pie`.

4.4 Adding Some Style: Line Colors, Markers, and More

In the previous section, we learned to make figures, which is great, but there definitely is some room for improvement. For example, all of the lines were blue, the lines were somewhat thin, and the font size for the text was also a bit small.

4.4.1 Colors

First, let's try and set some basic properties of lines: colors, markers, and styles.

MATLAB provides us with a few default colors: blue, green, red, black, and a handful of others. Importantly, these default colors can be accessed with single characters, such as 'b', 'g', 'r', and 'k' for the four colors just mentioned. To use these colors, we just need to specify one of these characters to the `bar`, `plot`, or `errorbar` function after the data.

```
1 >> bar(mAro,'g')
```

To get a bit more control, we can also set specific colors by providing values for the amount of red, green, and blue, with values between 0 and 1. For example, [0 0 0] would be black, [1 1 1] is white, and [0 .75 0] a relatively strong shade of green. To use these values, we need to tell MATLAB that we are actually specifying a color.

```
1 >> bar(mAro,'color',[0 .75 0])
```

In the case of bar graphs, we can specify colors for the edges and for the faces.

```
1 >> bar(mAro,'edgecolor',[.5 0 0],'facecolor',[.5 .5 1])
```

When specifying custom colors, some may find it easier to use hex codes, as in HTML colors (e.g., 'FFFFFF' is white). If you aren't sure what I'm referring to, feel free to skip over this example. There are many online color choosers that use hex codes for colors, so this is also quite convenient for specifying particular colors. To allow MATLAB to use hex colors, I have included my own function along with this book (`imbhex2color`).

```
1 >> bar(mAro,'facecolor',imbhex2color('91D2E2'))
```

4.4.2 Line Styles

'Styles' is probably not the most descriptive word, but here I am referring to lines that can be solid or dashed (Figure 4.8). Here we can specify lines to be solid, dashed, or only markers with -, --, or ., respectively, in the same way we specified the single-character colors. Other types of dashed lines can also be specified with : and :-.

```
1 >> plot(mAro,'-r')
2 >> plot(mAro,'--r')
3 >> plot(mAro,'.r')
4 >> plot(mAro,':r')
5 >> plot(mAro,':-r')
```

Figure 4.8   An example of a dashed line (--).

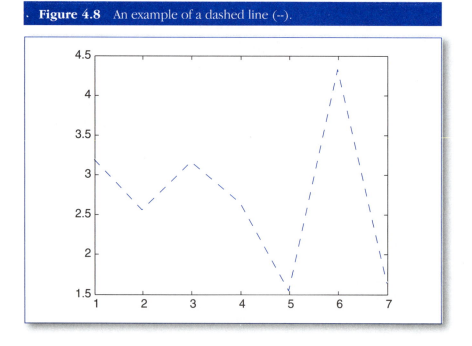

We can additionally adjust the width of our lines with the 'linewidth' property and the width of the bars in our bar graphs with the 'barwidth' property.

```
1 >> bar(mAro,'g','linewidth',3)
```

4.4.3 Markers

In case you aren't sure what I mean by "marker," I am referring to the dots that mark each data point in line graphs, as in Figure 4.9.

```
1 >> plot(mAro,'^r')
2 >> axis([0 8 1 9])
```

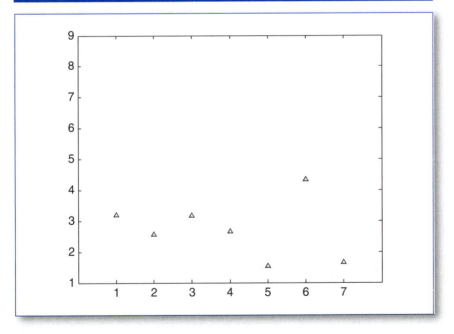

Figure 4.9 An example of a custom marker.

Here we have an upward-pointing triangle as our marker.

MATLAB provides us with a number of markers, most of which are listed below. Note that by default, markers are hollow, and their presence causes there to be no line between the markers. However, both of these settings can easily be changed.

MATLAB identifier	Example	Description
.	.	Dot
o	○	Circle
s	□	Square
^	△	Triangle (up)
v	▽	Triangle (down)
<	◁	Triangle (left)
>	▷	Triangle (right)
d	◇	Diamond
+	+	Cross (plus)
x	×	Cross (X)
p	★	Star
*	*	Asterisk

To adjust the color of the markers, and to give them a fill, we can specify these as well with the 'markerfacecolor' and 'markeredgecolor' line properties.

```
1 >> plot(mAro,'-s','markerfacecolor',[1 0 0],'markeredgecolor',[0 1 0])
```

We can also adjust the size of the markers with the property 'markersize'.

```
1 >> plot(mAro,'-s','markersize',5)
```

For more examples in MATLAB's own documentation, check doc linespec.

4.4.4 More Colors

To have more control over colors, you can also use the **colormap** function. Using this function, we access several color schemes built in MATLAB, as well as apply our own complex color schemes to figures. To see a list of the built-in color schemes, check doc colormap.

4.5 Multiple Graphs in the Same Figure

So far we have learned to make different kinds of graphs and customize them, but they are still relatively simple. We cannot yet plot multiple lines at the same time. The key command here is **hold on**. This tells MATLAB that we do *not* want to overwrite the current figure with the plot from the subsequent command, but rather we want to *hold* the current figure.

This is mostly used by behavioral researchers to overlay error bars on a bar graph (Figure 4.10). To give a simple example, let's first plot the arousal ratings for each word type, but we'll also use markers and colors.

```
1 >> bar(mAro,'facecolor',imbhex2color('91D2E2'))
2 >> hold on
3 >> errorbar(1:7,mAro,semAro,'.k','markersize',1)
4 >> axis([0 8 1 9])
5 >> set(gca,'XTickLabel',types)
6 >> xlabel('Word Type')
7 >> ylabel('Mean Rating')
8 >> title('Arousal')
9 >> hold off
```

If you look at the bottom of the figure, it looks like there is no bottom border where the bars are. This is an artifact of changing the axis boundaries to not include zero. This can easily be fixed in the figure by adding a line ourselves.

```
1 >> plot([0 8],[1 1],'k')
```

Figure 4.10   Our first bar graph with error bars.

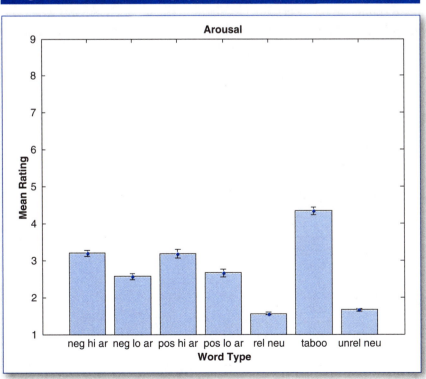

4.5.1 Opening and Closing Figures

While `hold` is great for plotting multiple figures on the same axes, at some point we will want to close the current figure and move on to the next. `hold off` can be used to tell MATLAB to stop using the same axes.

Even more useful to this purpose are `figure` and `close`. `figure` tells MATLAB to open a new figure window, while `close` will close the most recent figure window. `close all` can also be used to close *all* figure windows.

4.6 Legend—Wait for It— . . .

What if we wanted to include bars from multiple measures in the same figure? We would need a legend!

Let's try doing this with the tabooness measure. I'll save you the repetitiveness of calculating the means and SEMs for each word type; you can just copy them from me here. If you are so inclined, though, the calculations for the mean are the same as from page 69 and the SEMs from page 75, though here we would use column 14 (tabooness) rather than column 18 (arousal), as noted in `data_legend.txt` and at several places in the book. Hopefully, the column numbers will seem less arbitrary and more memorable when you are working with your own data. In the next chapter, we will learn how to automate more tedious analyses such as this.

```
1 >> mTab
2 mTab =
3     1.8304    1.5911    1.3407    1.0793    1.0490    4.8284    1.0966
4 >> semTab
5 semTab =
6     0.0802    0.0805    0.1072    0.0208    0.0142    0.1550    0.0143
```

If we plot them together on the same figure, we would get something like this.

```
1 >> bar((1:7)-.2,mAro,'facecolor',imbhex2color('91D2E2'), ...
2 'barwidth',.35)
3 >> hold on
4 >> bar((1:7)+.2,mTab,'facecolor',imbhex2color('E5E5E5'), ...
5 'barwidth',.35)
6 >> errorbar((1:7)-.2,mAro,semAro,'.k','markersize',1)
7 >> errorbar((1:7)+.2,mTab,semTab,'.k','markersize',1)
8 >> axis([0 8 1 9])
```

```
 9 >> set(gca,'XTick',1:7,'XTickLabel',types)
10 >> xlabel('Word Type')
11 >> ylabel('Mean Rating')
12 >> plot([0 8],[1 1],'k')
13 >> hold off
```

And now we probably should add a legend.

```
1 >> legend('Arousal','Tabooness')
```

As with all of the other figure-related functions, we can also set some additional options for the orientation (horizontal or vertical) and position. For the legend position, the simplest locations we can provide are "north", "south", "east", and "west", as well as all corner directions (e.g., "northwest"). We can also remove the box around the legend using legend box-off; now see Figure 4.11. For further details, see doc legend.

Figure 4.11   Mean ratings of both arousal and tabooness for all word types.

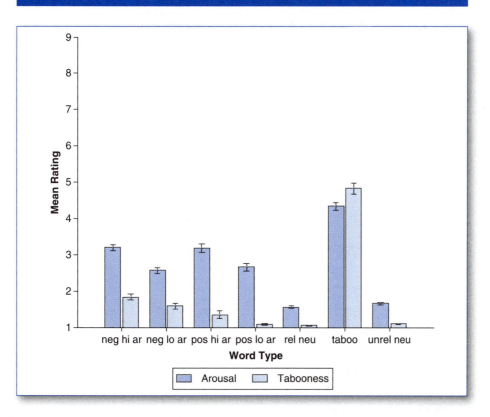

```
1 >> legend('Arousal','Tabooness','orientation','horizontal', ...
2 'location','northwest')
3 >> legend boxoff
```

Reminder: I used "…" on one line. This allows us to continue the command on the next line. Normally, I would not use this myself; however, the line otherwise did not fit within the width of the code box printed in the book. (Also see Tip #2 on page 6.)

4.7 More Advanced Axis and Figure Customization

Earlier, we mentioned a special type of object called gca, which stands for "get current axes." In other words, with gca we can set properties of the axes, such as the locations of the axis tick marks as was done before.

We can also specify the font size and font weight (i.e., bold), with the coding being relatively the same as with the other commands.

```
1 >> set(gca,'fontsize',14)
```

We can also set the properties of the labels directly, if we first assign them to a variable.

```
1 >> a=xlabel('Word Type');
2 >> b=ylabel('Mean Rating');
3 >> set(a,'fontsize',20,'fontweight','bold')
4 >> set(b,'fontsize',20,'fontweight','bold')
```

Another noteworthy figure property is tick direction. MATLAB has ticks pointing inward by default. You may not have noticed this earlier, but sometimes the little details can make a figure look that much better. Take a look at the figures on the last few pages and see what you think. To switch the direction of the ticks to instead point outward, you just need a single line of code.

```
1 >> set(gca,'TickDir','out')
```

★ TIP #29

You can also adjust the 'TickLength'! ■

4.7.1 Transparent Backgrounds

If you want to have a transparent background for your figure, such as for use in a presentation, you will need to set the background color of the figure to 'none'. (Kind of makes sense, no?)

```
1 >> set(gca,'Color','none')
```

4.8 To Have More Lines or Too Many Lines?

Apart from plotting our data as lines or bars, figures also involve other features/properties that are important, such as boxes and grid lines. In this section, we will learn about some of the more common of these figure properties.

One important type of box is the one that can be used to border the figure on all sides. Most of the figures shown in this chapter included a box around the figure, as this is the MATLAB default, but Figure 4.12 did not. This can be achieved using the box function.

```
1 >> box on
2 >> box off
```

Grid lines can also be added or removed from figures using the MATLAB function grid.

```
1 >> grid on
2 >> grid off
```

> ★ TIP #30
>
> You can also add multiple plots to the same figure window using the function subplot. Annotations can also be easily added to figures using text and rectangle. ■

In Figure 4.12, we used a few more of these finishing touches to try and improve on Figure 4.11. What do you think? Below is the code for this final version.

```
 1 >> bar((1:7)-.2,mAro,'facecolor',imbhex2color('91D2E2'), ...
 2 'barwidth',.35)
 3 >> hold on
 4 >> bar((1:7)+.2,mTab,'facecolor',imbhex2color('E5E5E5'), ...
 5 'barwidth',.35)
 6 >> errorbar((1:7)-.2,mAro,semAro,'.k','markersize',1)
 7 >> errorbar((1:7)+.2,mTab,semTab,'.k','markersize',1)
 8 >> axis([0 8 1 9])
 9 >> set(gca,'XTick',1:7)
10 >> set(gca,'XTickLabel',types)
11 >> plot([0 8],[1 1],'k')
12 >> legend('Arousal','Tabooness')
13 >> legend boxoff
14 >> set(gca,'fontsize',10)
15 >> a=xlabel('Word Type');
16 >> b=ylabel('Mean Rating');
17 >> set(a,'fontsize',14,'fontweight','bold')
18 >> set(b,'fontsize',14,'fontweight','bold')
19 >> set(gca,'TickDir','out')
20 >> box off
21 >> hold off
```

Figure 4.12   The final figure.

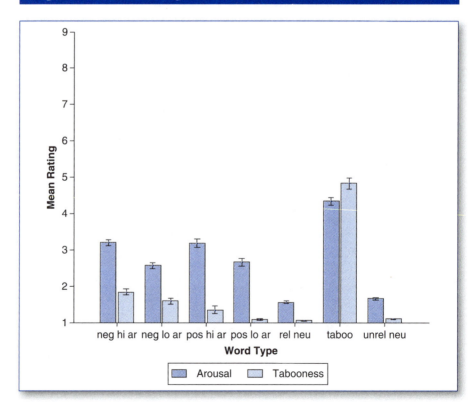

4.9 Making Three-Dimensional Figures

MATLAB also allows us to make three-dimensional figures fairly easily, though they also tend to get a bit harder to interpret.

For example, Figure 4.13 illustrates a three-dimensional bar graph made with `bar3`, generated with the code below.

```
1 >> bar3([mAro;mTab])
2 >> xlabel('Word Type')
3 >> zlabel('Mean Rating')
4 >> set(gca,'XTickLabel',types)
5 >> set(gca,'YTickLabel',{'Arousal','Tabooness'})
6 >> set(gca,'ZTick',1:9)
7 >> axis([0 7.5 .5 3 1 9])
```

Figure 4.13   Trying out a three-dimensional bar graph.

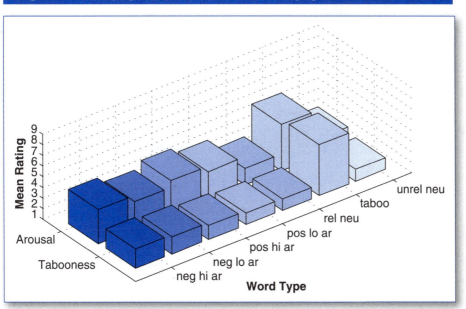

Personally, I don't use three-dimensional figures, but they nonetheless may be useful in your own work. Other types of three-dimensional figures can be made using `plot3`, `scatter3`, and `mesh`.

EXERCISES

Let's take the training wheels off and try out some of the new functions and operations that we learned in this chapter!

1. Make a simple horizontal bar graph (e.g., no custom colors or changes to the axis ranges) of the mean imageability ratings for each word type from the `worddb` data set.

2. Make a pair of bars (as in Figure 4.12 [page 88]) for the familiarity and personal use ratings. Include SEM error bars.

3. Remake the scatterplot of Valence × Arousal shown in Figure 4.7 (p. 78), but use different colors and markers for each word type. Be sure to also include a legend!

4. Adjust your code from Question 3 to make a scatterplot of the Tabooness × Offensiveness ratings.

5. The `iqbrain` study intentionally included a high-IQ and a low-IQ group, rather than having IQ as a continuous variable. Determine the IQ range for each group and illustrate this in a plot. Mark the highest and lowest IQs in each group (i.e., the range) with error bars, rather than calculating the SEM.

6. Add triangle-shaped markers (i.e., ∇ and Δ) to your figure from Question 5 for the highest and lowest IQs in each group.

See page 198 for the solutions. Now you are beginning to be quite capable in MATLAB! Next, we will learn to automate our analyses to make it easier to analyze a full data set!

FUNCTION REVIEW

Plot types: `bar barh plot errorbar scatter image colorbar imagesc contour pie`

General figure: `xlabel ylabel title axis print hold legend figure close box grid set` (XTick, YTick, XTickLabel, FontSize, FontWeight, TickDir, Color)

Plot properties: `Color   LineSpec   FaceColor   LineWidth   BarWidth   MarkerSize MarkerFaceColor MarkerEdgeColor`

5

AUTOMATING YOUR ANALYSES

So far we've learned how to do a wide variety of tasks with commands, including loading data (Chapter 2), doing basic descriptive statistics (such as calculating the mean and standard deviation; Chapter 3), and making figures (Chapter 4). However, as of yet, you have always had to type the commands each time or perhaps copy and paste them from another program into MATLAB. This chapter will bring an end to the tedium! First, we will make a script, then learn how to make it more dynamic with conditional statements and for loops, and finally learn to make our own custom functions.

5.1 Your First Script

In the previous chapters, there have been quite a few lines of code for you to type by hand. Hopefully, you followed along with most of these, as trying the commands yourself will go a long way to learning the MATLAB functions yourself. However, considering that MATLAB is made for running complex analyses, hopefully you are waiting for me to show you a better way to run commands in MATLAB. Well, you'll be glad to know about scripts. Briefly, scripts are multiple lines of commands that are saved into a simple text file so they can be easily run by just typing the name of the script file in MATLAB. Scripts can be as short or as long as you want, a mere three or four lines or easily several hundred lines of commands.

To make a script, use the MATLAB function `edit`. You can also specify particular file names to edit (or create and then edit) in the form of `edit('filename')`. The file extension of these script files will always be `.m`. As an example, I have included a short script based on one of the figures made in the previous chapter, called `mkfigAro.m`, in the same folder as the word database data set.

```
1 >> mkfigAro
```

For your convenience, I have also copied the contents of this script file below.

```
 1 fid = fopen ('JanschewitzB386appB.txt','r');
 2 formatstring = ['%s %s' repmat (' %f', 1, 19) ];
 3 worddata=textscan(fid, formatstring, 'headerlines',5, 'delimiter','\t');
 4 fclose(fid);
 5
 6 types = unique (worddata{2}-(1: 460));
 7 i=1;
 8 mAro(i)=mean(worddata{18}(find(strcmp(worddata{2},types{i}))));
 9 stdAro(i)=std(worddata{18}(find(strcmp(worddata{2},types{i}))));
10 nword(i)=sum(strcmp(worddata{2},types{i}));
11 i=i+1;
12 mAro(i)=mean(worddata{18}(find(strcmp(worddata{2},types{i}))));
13 stdAro(i)=std(worddata{18}(find(strcmp(worddata{2},types{i}))));
14 nWord(i)=sum(strcmp(worddata{2},types{i}));
15 i=i+1;
16 mAro(i)=mean(worddata{18}(find(strcmp(worddata{2},types{i}))));
17 stdAro(i)=std(worddata{18}(find(strcmp(worddata{2},types{i}))));
18 nWord(i)=sum(strcmp(worddata{2},types{i}));
19 i=i+1;
20 mAro(i)=mean(worddata{18}(find(strcmp(worddata{2},types{i}))));
21 stdAro(i)=std(worddata{18}(find(strcmp(worddata{2},types{i}))));
22 nWord(i)=sum(strcmp(worddata{2},types{i}));
23 i=i+1;
24 mAro(i)=mean(worddata{18}(find(strcmp(worddata{2},types{i}))));
25 stdAro(i)=std(worddata{18}(find(strcmp(worddata{2}, types{i}))));
26 nWord(i)=sum(strcmp(worddata{2},types{i}));
27 i=i+1;
28 mAro(i)=mean(worddata{18}(find(strcmp(worddata{2},types{i}))));
29 stdAro(i)=std(worddata{18}(find(strcmp(worddata{2}, types{i}))));
30 nWord(i)=sum(strcmp(worddata{2},types{i}));
31 i=i+1;
32 mAro(i)=mean(worddata{18}(find(strcmp(worddata{2},types{i}))));
33 stdAro(i)=std(worddata{18}(find(strcmp(worddata{2},types{i}))));
34 nWord(i)=sum(strcmp(worddata{2},types{i}));
35 semAro = stdAro./sqrt(nWord);
36
37 bar(mAro,'facecolor',imbhex2color('91D2E2'))
38 hold on
39 errorbar(1:7,mAro,semAro,'.k','markersize' ,1)
40 axis ([0 8 1 9])
41 set(gca ,'XTickLabel ',types)
```

```
42 set(gca,'TickDir','out')
43 xlabel('Word Type')
44 ylabel('Mean Rating')
45 title('Arousal')
46 plot([0 8],[1 1],'k')
47 box off
48 hold off
```

Try running `mkfigAro.m` and see how simple it is! Sorry I waited so long to share this one with you; I needed to wait until you knew enough commands for it to make sense and be worthwhile.

5.1.1 ECHO, Echo, echo

One potential downside of using a script is that sometimes you might not see which lines of code are outputting values (e.g., if you didn't have semicolons in certain places). To have MATLAB print all of the commands it executes as it runs them, you can use the echo function.

In `mkfigAro2.m`, I adjusted a few lines to output values as you go. Try running this script without echo on and then with echo.

```
 1 >> mkfigAro2
 2 worddata =
 3    Columns 1 through 4
 4     {464x1 cell}    {464x1 cell}    [464x1 double]    [464x1 double]
 5    Columns 5 through 8
 6     [464x1 double]    [464x1 double]    [464x1 double]    [464x1 double]
 7    Columns 9 through 12
 8     [464x1 double]    [464x1 double]    [464x1 double]    [464x1 double]
 9    Columns 13 through 16
10     [464x1 double]    [464x1 double]    [464x1 double]    [464x1 double]
11    Columns 17 through 20
12     [464x1 double]    [464x1 double]    [464x1 double]    [464x1 double]
13    Column 21
14     [463x1 double]
15 types =
16     'neg hi ar'
17     'neg lo ar'
18     'pos hi ar'
19     'pos lo ar'
20     'rel neu'
21     'taboo'
```

(Continued)

(Continued)

```
22    'unrel neu'
23 mAro =
24    3.1987    2.5715    3.1730    2.6630    1.5595    4.3357    1.6551
25 stdAro =
26    0.5304    0.5505    0.8005    0.6961    0.2930    0.9896    0.3070
27 semAro =
28    0.0782    0.0812    0.1180    0.1026    0.0305    0.1032    0.0320
29 >> echo on
30 >> mkfigAro2
31 fid = fopen('JanschewitzB386appB.txt','r');
32 formatstring = [ '%s %s' repmat(' %f ',1,19) ];
33 worddata=textscan(fid,formatstring,'headerlines',5,'delimiter','\t')
34 worddata =
35   Columns 1 through 4
36    {464x1 cell}    {464x1 cell}    [464x1 double]    [464x1 double]
37   Columns 5 through 8
38    [464x1 double]    [464x1 double]    [464x1 double]    [464x1 double]
39   Columns 9 through 12
40    [464x1 double]    [464x1 double]    [464x1 double]    [464x1 double]
41   Columns 13 through 16
42    [464x1 double]    [464x1 double]    [464x1 double]    [464x1 double]
43   Columns 17 through 20
44    [464x1 double]    [464x1 double]    [464x1 double]    [464x1 double]
45   Column 21
46    [463x1 double]
47 fclose(fid);
48 types=unique(worddata{2}(1:460))
49 types =
50    'neg hi ar'
51    'neg lo ar'
52    'pos hi ar'
53    'pos lo ar'
54    'rel neu'
55    'taboo'
56    'unrel neu'
57 i=1;
58 mAro(i)=mean(worddata{18}(find(strcmp(worddata{2},types{i}))));
59 stdAro(i)=std(worddata{18}(find(strcmp(worddata{2},types{i}))));
60 nWord(i)=sum(strcmp(worddata{2},types{i}));
61 i=i+1;
62 mAro(i)=mean(worddata{18}(find(strcmp(worddata{2},types{i}))));
63 stdAro(i)=std(worddata{18}(find(strcmp(worddata{2},types{i}))));
64 nWord(i)=sum(strcmp(worddata{2},types{i}));
65 i=i+1;
66 mAro(i)=mean(worddata{18}(find(strcmp(worddata{2},types{i}))));
```

```
67  stdAro(i)=std(worddata{18}(find(strcmp(worddata{2},types{i}))));
68  nWord(i)=sum(strcmp(worddata{2},types{i}));
69  i=i+1;
70  mAro(i)=mean(worddata{18}(find(strcmp(worddata{2},types{i}))));
71  stdAro(i)=std(worddata{18}(find(strcmp(worddata{2},types{i}))));
72  nWord(i)=sum(strcmp(worddata{2},types{i}));
73  i=i+1;
74  mAro(i)=mean(worddata{18}(find(strcmp(worddata{2},types{i}))));
75  stdAro(i)=std(worddata{18}(find(strcmp(worddata{2},types{i}))));
76  nWord(i)=sum(strcmp(worddata{2},types{i}));
77  i=i+1;
78  mAro(i)=mean(worddata{18}(find(strcmp(worddata{2},types{i}))));
79  stdAro(i)=std(worddata{18}(find(strcmp(worddata{2},types{i}))));
80  nWord(i)=sum(strcmp(worddata{2},types{i}));
81  i=i+1;
82  mAro(i)=mean(worddata{18}(find(strcmp(worddata{2},types{i}))));
83  stdAro(i)=std(worddata{18}(find(strcmp(worddata{2},types{i}))));
84  nWord(i)=sum(strcmp(worddata{2},types{i}));
85  mAro
86  mAro =
87     3.1987    2.5715    3.1730    2.6630    1.5595    4.3357    1.6551
88  stdAro
89  stdAro =
90     0.5304    0.5505    0.8005    0.6961    0.2930    0.9896    0.3070
91  semAro = stdAro./sqrt(nWord)
92  semAro =
93     0.0782    0.0812    0.1180    0.1026    0.0305    0.1032    0.0320
94  bar(mAro,'facecolor',imbhex2color('91D2E2'))
95  hold on
96  errorbar(1:7,mAro,semAro,'.k','markersize',1)
97  axis([0 8 1 9])
98  set(gca,'XTickLabel',types)
99  set(gca,'TickDir','out')
100 xlabel('Word Type')
101 ylabel('Mean Rating')
102 title('Arousal')
103 plot([0 8],[1 1],'k')
104 box off
105 hold off
106 >> echo off
```

5.2 Comments

Now that we can easily store many lines of MATLAB commands for later use, it would be good if we could also remember what they were for! This can be done with *comments* mixed in with the code. In MATLAB, comments are denoted by preceding the comment with a percent (%) sign. Comments are especially important if you later share your code with others.

```
1 % I can write whatever I want and MATLAB can't hear me!
```

Comments can also be useful when testing your code; comment out a block of code that you know works and just focus on the code that you are still developing. You can comment blocks of text using %{ and end this block comment with %}.

```
1 %{
2 This is not going to get run by MATLAB.
3 %}
```

5.3 Conditional Statements

Now that we are making scripts, there may be instances where we only want to run part of the script at a given time, such as if you easily want to disable a block of code in a dynamic way, rather than simply commenting it out. For instance, you may want to redo some calculations, but not always remake the corresponding figure that's also in the same script. The basic logic of conditional statements is if-elseif-else.

```
1 if condition1
2     % do something
3 elseif condition2
4     % do something else
5 elseif condition3
6     % do some other thing
7 else
8     % if all else fails, what should we do?
9 end
```

Basically, we are telling MATLAB that if some specific condition is met (condition1; i.e., a comparison/Boolean statement), then we should "do something." If this condition is not met, MATLAB moves on to the next condition, here condition2, and checks if that condition is met. If not, MATLAB then moves to condition3. This process can be continued indefinitely, but at the end you can include a last block of code to accommodate if no previous condition was met, using just `else` (though this isn't necessary). Finally, we end with `end`, so MATLAB knows that this set of conditional statements is complete and that the rest of the code is not part of the conditions.

For a more concrete example, see this edited portion of `mkfigAro2.m` that uses conditional statements based on the new variable `genFig`.

```
1 genFig = 0;
2
3 fid = fopen('JanschewitzB386appB.txt','r');
4 formatstring = [ '%s %s' repmat(' %f',1,19)];
5 worddata=textscan(fid,formatstring,'headerlines',5,'delimiter','\t')
6 fclose(fid);
7
8 % the code for types, mAro, stdAro, nWord, and semAro, would go here,
9 % I just removed it for brevity
10
11 if genFig == 1
12     bar(mAro,'facecolor',imbhex2color('91D2E2'))
13     hold on
14     errorbar(1:7,mAro,semAro,'.k','markersize',1)
15     axis([0 8 1 9])
16     set(gca,'XTickLabel',types)
17     set(gca,'TickDir','out')
18     xlabel('Word Type')
19     ylabel('Mean Rating')
20     title('Arousal')
21     plot([0 8],[1 1],'k')
22     box off
23     hold off
24 else
25     % do nothing
26 end
```

★ TIP #31

If you find yourself nesting multiple `if` statements within each other, you may also want to look into `switch-case-otherwise` statements. ∎

5.4 Looping Through the Repetition

Notice how there are lines of code you end up using repetitively? For instance, in `mkfigAro2.m`, we have this giant block of code (below) that we need to get the mean and standard deviations for the arousal ratings, and word counts, for each word type.

```
 1 i=1;
 2 mAro(i)=mean(worddata{18}(find(strcmp(worddata{2},types{i}))));
 3 stdAro(i)=std(worddata{18}(find(strcmp(worddata{2},types{i}))));
 4 nWord(i)=sum(strcmp(worddata{2},types{i}));
 5 i=i+1;
 6 mAro(i)=mean(worddata{18}(find(strcmp(worddata{2},types{i}))));
 7 stdAro(i)=std(worddata{18}(find(strcmp(worddata{2},types{i}))));
 8 nWord(i)=sum(strcmp(worddata{2},types{i}));
 9 i=i+1;
10 mAro(i)=mean(worddata{18}(find(strcmp(worddata{2},types{i}))));
11 stdAro(i)=std(worddata{18}(find(strcmp(worddata{2},types{i}))));
12 nWord(i)=sum(strcmp(worddata{2},types{i}));
13 i=i+1;
14 mAro(i)=mean(worddata{18}(find(strcmp(worddata{2},types{i}))));
15 stdAro(i)=std(worddata{18}(find(strcmp(worddata{2},types{i}))));
16 nWord(i)=sum(strcmp(worddata{2},types{i}));
17 i=i+1;
18 mAro(i)=mean(worddata{18}(find(strcmp(worddata{2},types{i}))));
19 stdAro(i)=std(worddata{18}(find(strcmp(worddata{2},types{i}))));
20 nWord(i)=sum(strcmp(worddata{2},types{i}));
21 i=i+1;
22 mAro(i)=mean(worddata{18}(find(strcmp(worddata{2},types{i}))));
23 stdAro(i)=std(worddata{18}(find(strcmp(worddata{2},types{i}))));
24 nWord(i)=sum(strcmp(worddata{2},types{i}));
25 i=i+1;
26 mAro(i)=mean(worddata{18}(find(strcmp(worddata{2},types{i}))));
27 stdAro(i)=std(worddata{18}(find(strcmp(worddata{2},types{i}))));
28 nWord(i)=sum(strcmp(worddata{2},types{i}));
```

Hopefully, you've been thinking this looks really clumsy. It is. Wouldn't it be wonderful if we could somehow *loop* through these lines, *for* each word type? If so, you've come to the right place!

In essence, a `for` loop allows you to cycle through a block of code while changing one variable to a different value each time you go through it. The code above was somewhat written with this logic in mind, but we had to take our time to gradually work up to this.

Let's start with something simple. Try running this code:

```
1 for i=1:10
2     i
3 end
```

MATLAB should respond with this:

```
 1 i =
 2        1
 3 i =
 4        2
 5 i =
 6        3
 7 i =
 8        4
 9 i =
10        5
11 i =
12        6
13 i =
14        7
15 i =
16        8
17 i =
18        9
19 i =
20       10
```

Ta-da! Your very first for loop. A loop is simply a way to cycle through a series of commands, while changing *one* thing: the variable we loop through. We can also vary our step size, such that we don't go though every value in a range, using techniques we learned back in Chapter 1 (p. 8).

Code:

```
1 for i=1:2:10
2 i
3 end
```

Output:

```
 1 i =
 2        1
 3 i =
 4        3
 5 i =
 6        5
 7 i =
 8        7
 9 i =
10        9
```

Code:

```
1 for i=0:10:100
2 i
3 end
```

Output:

```
 1 i =
 2          0
 3 i =
 4         10
 5 i =
 6         20
 7 i =
 8         30
 9 i =
10         40
11 i =
12         50
13 i =
14         60
15 i =
16         70
17 i =
18         80
19 i =
20         90
21 i =
22        100
```

Let's look at how a `for` loop works, and illustrate this block of code in Figure 5.1

Now, let's step things up. What if we could replace that large code block with the means and standard deviations with just a few lines? And no, we won't be just removing a bunch of line breaks. This code will function identically to the previous large code block.

```
1 for i=1:length(types)
2     mAro(i)=mean(worddata{18}(find(strcmp(worddata{2},types{i}))));
3     stdAro(i)=std(worddata{18}(find(strcmp(worddata{2},types{i}))));
4     nWord(i)=sum(strcmp(worddata{2},types{i}));
5 end
```

Figure 5.1 Illustrated logic of a `for` loop. The general logic is displayed on the left, with a specific example shown on the right. Code in the black rectangles is not explicitly given to MATLAB, but instead occurs "automatically" as part of the `for` loop.

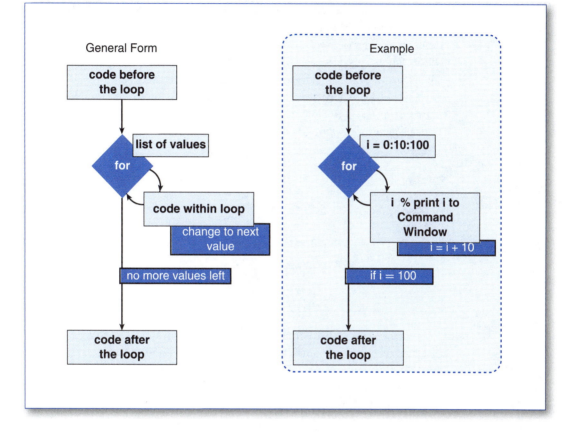

Give it a try! Take a look at the `mkfigAro3.m` file and see it in action.

★ **TIP #32**

`for` loops aren't the only type of loop. `while` loops can also be quite useful and are more general purpose than a `for` loop ■

5.5 Initializing a New Matrix

In the for loops we've been making in this chapter, the length of a variable increases on each cycle of the loop. First, it only has one value, and by the end, it would have seven. When we're working with relatively small lengths like these, MATLAB can expand the variable's size relatively easily. However, if we end up working with much larger variables, MATLAB will be slowed down by the act of increasing the amount of computer memory allocated to the variable. This can easily be remedied though, by creating a matrix of the "final" size before we start, and then filling in the contents through the for loop, as before. There are a few ways to do to this, such as to initialize a new matrix composed only of **zeros** or only of **ones**. The syntax for these two options is fairly straightforward:

```
1 >> zeros(1,7)
2 ans =
3      0    0    0    0    0    0    0
4 >> ones(1,7)
5 ans =
6      1    1    1    1    1    1    1
7 >> ones(2,3)
8 ans =
9      1    1    1
10     1    1    1
```

Another choice is to create a matrix of random numbers from a uniform distribution ranging from 0 to 1 using the **rand** function. Large matrices of random numbers can be quite useful when creating an initial matrix for computational modeling. What best suits your needs varies based on what you need the matrix initialized for.

```
1 >> rand(4,5)
2 ans =
3     0.8147    0.6324    0.9575    0.9572    0.4218
4     0.9058    0.0975    0.9649    0.4854    0.9157
5     0.1270    0.2785    0.1576    0.8003    0.7922
6     0.9134    0.5469    0.9706    0.1419    0.9595
```

★ **TIP #33**

If **rand** looks interesting, you may also want to look into **randn** and **randperm**. ■

If you'd rather not create a matrix of actual numbers, you may want to instead consider using the nan function to create a matrix of NaNs.

```
1 >> nan(3,5)
2 ans =
3    NaN    NaN    NaN    NaN    NaN
4    NaN    NaN    NaN    NaN    NaN
5    NaN    NaN    NaN    NaN    NaN
```

In other cases, you may need a placeholder that isn't just one repeating number. Note that you can always get any number as a placeholder by multiplying the desired number by ones. If you need a repeating sequence combined with your data, what you need is repmat, a function we previously covered in Section 2.6.3.

5.6 Putting It Into Practice

While the example data sets we have used thus far were chosen to be comparable to that which you would use yourself, there was one key difference: You usually will have separate data files for each individual participant. For loops are perfect for this situation, where we would put the code for loading and analyzing the individual subject data within the for loop.

Let's try this out with a new example data set.

5.6.1 A New Data Set

In a study by Bogacz, Hu, Holmes, and Cohen (2010; Experiment 1), participants were shown an array of dots on a computer screen. On each trial, a proportion of these dots were shifted ('moved') either to the left or right side of the screen, while the remaining dots were randomly repositioned. Participants were asked to judge whether the dots predominately moved to the left or to the right, that is, a two-alternative forced choice (2-AFC) motion discrimination/decision-making task. Between blocks of trials, the delay between the offset of one trial and the onset of the next trial was experimentally manipulated to be 0.5, 1, or 2 seconds. The dependent variables were error rate (i.e., $1 - $ accuracy; higher error rates mean more incorrect responses/worse accuracy) and reaction time. In one condition, there was also an increased delay after incorrect responses (delay penalty). Additionally, participants were paid 1 cent for each correct response to increase motivation.

Though Bogacz et al. (2010) used this task along with a computational model to test for effects of the delay on speed-accuracy trade-offs, here we will focus only on the behavioral data itself. Feel free to look at the original paper for more details on the experimental design.

Data from this experiment can be found in the **decision1** folder within the book's data folder, and is already in **.mat** format, as provided by the first author of the study.

5.6.2 Practicing Our Basic Analyses

Before we get ahead of ourselves too much, let's load in the data for just one subject and take a look at what variables we have to work with.

```
1 >> load('subject401')
2 >> who
3 Your variables are:
4 D          ER       ST          money
5 Dpen       RT       blocknum    trialnum
```

We can also use the **whos** to get a bit more information about these variables.

```
 1 >> whos
 2    Name        Size        Bytes    Class       Attributes
 3    D           1x1130       9040    double
 4    Dpen        1x1130       9040    double
 5    ER          1x1130       1130    logical
 6    RT          1x1130       9040    double
 7    ST          1x1130       1130    logical
 8    blocknum    1x1130       9040    double
 9    money       1x1             8    double
10    trialnum    1x1130       9040    double
```

The main benefit of **whos** is that it allows us to easily see the size of all variables as well as their format ('class')—which are all numbers.

Though the variable names are already fairly easy to interpret, descriptions of the variables were also provided with the data. These descriptions can be found in the **data_legend.txt** file in the same folder as the data and have also been included here.

```
 1 blocknum - number of block within the experiment, during which the trial
 2          was performed
 3 trialnum - number of trial within the block
 4 D - the delay between the response on this trial and onset of the
 5    next trial
 6 Dpen - additional penalty delay for making an error
 7 ST - binary vector describing the stimulus on the given trial,
 8    i.e. whether dots were moving leftwards or rightwards
 9 ER - binary vector describing whether participant made
10    incorrect response on this trial
11 RT - reaction time on the given trial [in seconds]
```

Okay, let's try something simple first: What was the mean error rate and reaction time for this participant, regardless of experimental condition?

```
1 >> mean(ER)
2 ans =
3     0.2469
4 >> mean(RT)
5 ans =
6     0.7521
```

Now, we know that this participant was incorrect on about a quarter of all trials and on average took about three-fourths of a second to respond. Of course, the experiment really had few conditions and was designed to test for speed-accuracy trade-offs in decision making. In this experiment, there were four conditions: (1) delay = 0.5 s, (2) delay = 1 s, (3) delay = 2 s, and (4) delay = 0.5 s with a delay penalty of 1.5 s. Let's start with getting the error rate and reaction time for Condition 1.

```
1 >> ERsub(1) = mean(ER(find(D==.5 & Dpen==0)))
2 ERsub =
3     0.2882
4 >> RTsub(1) = mean(RT(find(D==.5 & Dpen==0)))
5 RTsub =
6     0.6940
```

Hopefully, those lines of code make sense. If not, you may want to take another look at Section 3.7. I stored these values in index 1 of ERsub and RTsub to denote that they are the subject means for Condition 1. See if you can get the mean error rates and reaction times for the remaining three conditions, and store them in the appropriate indices of ERsub and RTsub, respectively.

How did you do? Does your attempt look similar to this?

```
 1 >> ERsub(2) = mean(ER(find(D==1 & Dpen==0)))
 2 ERsub =
 3      0.2882      0.2092
 4 >> ERsub(3) = mean(ER(find(D==2 & Dpen==0)))
 5 ERsub =
 6      0.2882      0.2092      0.2020
 7 >> ERsub(4) = mean(ER(find(D==.5 & Dpen==1.5)))
 8 ERsub =
 9      0.2882      0.2092      0.2020      0.2794
10 >> RTsub(2) = mean(RT(find(D==1 & Dpen==0)))
11 RTsub =
12      0.6940      0.7432
13 >> RTsub(3) = mean(RT(find(D==2 & Dpen==0)))
14 RTsub =
15      0.6940      0.7432      0.8165
16 >> RTsub(4) = mean(RT(find(D==.5 & Dpen==1.5)))
17 RTsub =
18      0.6940      0.7432      0.8165      0.7651
```

You can see that across the first three conditions, as the delay interval increased, the participant made fewer errors and was also slower (i.e., a speed-accuracy trade-off). In comparing Conditions 1 and 4, both of which have the same delay, the participant performed slightly better when there was the delay penalty (Condition 4), but reaction times suffered.

5.6.3 Automating Analyses Across Participants

Now, it's time to move on from this individual participant and try automating these analyses to be conducted on all 20 participants. Our first hurdle is to figure out how to automate the load-ing of participants' data. At the beginning of this section, we just asked MATLAB to load this particular subject by specifying the subject's file directly, but that won't work if we want to try using a for loop to load the data for all of the participants.

for loops and cell arrays (almost like "fruit loops and celery"?)

If we had fewer participants, we could try having a cell array consisting of the participants' file names. This isn't a particularly good solution in our current situation, but let's take a look at how that would work anyway. To test that the code is actually loading the data from each participant, we can also get the number of trials that that participant had, as this was not a fixed number for all participants in this experiment.

Here's the code for this "solution":

```
1 fnames={'subject401','subject402','subject403','subject404', ...
2 'subject405'};
3
4 for sub = 1:5
5     load(fnames{sub})
6     nTrial(sub) = length(ER);
7 end
8
9 nTrial
```

And the output is as follows:

```
1 nTrial =
2           1130        1351        1054        1169        1136
```

It looks like this would work, but it's clumsy and tedious, exactly what we are using MATLAB to avoid.

If we're a bit more creative, we can rework our code to make it a bit more optimal: We can remove the redundant portion of the file names that is consistent across all participants, and we can make the `for` loop cycle based on the number of file names provided.

```
1 fnames = {'01','02','03','04','05'};
2
3 for sub = 1:length(fnames)
4     load(['subject4' fnames{sub}])
5     nTrial(sub) = length(ER);
6 end
7
8 nTrial
```

The output is the same as before. This version is definitely better, but it's silly that we have to make a list of all of our participant numbers. Wouldn't it be better if we could construct the file name, a string, based on a number? Of course, MATLAB has a function for this—`sprintf`.

`sprintf` is made for constructing strings based on values stored in variables and is particularly useful if these values are numbers. Let's give this a try, using the `%f` formatting notation we learned earlier.

```
1 >> sub = 2;
2 >> sprintf('%f', sub)
3 ans =
4 2.000000
```

Not bad, but definitely could use some work. Let's tinker a bit and see what we can come up with. To learn more about the possible formatting available in sprintf, use doc.

```
1 >> sprintf('%.0f',sub)
2 ans =
3 2
4 >> sprintf('%02.0f',sub)
5 ans =
6 02
7 >> sprintf('subject4%02.0f',sub)
8 ans =
9 subject402
```

Much better! So all the code we really need from here is just these two lines:

```
1 >> sub = 2;
2 >> sprintf('subject4%02.0f',sub)
3 ans =
4 subject402
```

Now, let's try sprintf with our previous for loop, along with the appropriate changes.

```
1 lastsub = 5;
2
3 for sub = 1:lastsub
4     load(sprintf('subject4%02.0f',sub))
5     nTrial(sub) = length(ER);
6 end
7
8 nTrial
```

This version is pretty good now! Nonetheless, it is important to realize that in MATLAB there are often many ways to implement your desired analysis. Sometimes, there are slight advantages to one approach over another, and other times, they may be functionally identical. Sometimes, it's even good to try and implement an analysis in multiple ways to test if they are actually equivalent.

Skipping over missing subject numbers

In some cases, you may end up skipping over or excluding certain subject numbers in your `for` loop–driven analysis. As an example, maybe some participants never showed up for the experimental session, but you still want to attribute a subject number to them. It also may be that you simply want to exclude them from further analyses after finding that they performed poorly (e.g., below chance) in a preliminary analysis. These situations can easily be accommodated by using the `setdiff` function that we briefly covered earlier. Let's take a look.

```
 1 sublist = 1:5;
 2 skipped = 4;
 3
 4 sublist = setdiff(sublist,skipped);
 5
 6 for sub = sublist
 7     load(sprintf('subject4%02.0f',sub))
 8     nTrial(sub) = length(ER);
 9 end
10
11 nTrial
12 nTrial(sublist)
```

Notice now that the output here is as follows:

```
1 nTrial =
2          1130          1351          1054             0          1136
3 ans =
4          1130          1351          1054          1136
```

Even though we skipped over subject number 4, it still holds an index in the `nTrial` variable. However, MATLAB automatically filled in a value at this position because we never specified anything and instead just skipped over to subject number 5. If we instead only look at `nTrial(sublist)`, listed in the above output as `ans`, we still are able to see only the values corresponding to IDs that actually correspond to our data. This is perfectly fine to do; you just need to make sure you remember this when you do your further analyses, such as calculating the mean. Here's an example:

```
1 >> mean(nTrial)
2 ans =
3    934.2000
4 >>mean(nTrial(sublist))
5 ans =
6    1.1678e+03
```

Remember to be careful with this; accidentally averaging zeros into your results can make a big difference! When in doubt, take a look at the values going into your analyses directly (e.g., **nTrial**) and make sure they make sense to you.

> ★ **TIP #34**
>
> When you are working with your own data, you probably won't want to keep the data and your analysis scripts in the same folder. When you're using the `load` function, it is easy to include the path as well, such as `load (sprintf ('../data/subject4%02.0f',sub))` to go up from the current directory and into a "data" folder. This is generally a good practice, but try not to call any of your variables path, as `path` is also a function in MATLAB. ∎

Advanced: Smart `for` Loops Using `dir`

Back in Chapter 2, we learned that `dir` can be used to list the contents of a directory. However, it can do much more: We can store the directory list in a variable for use with our code as well! However, the output of `dir` is yet another type of variable: a structure. Structures can be quite complicated, hence this subsection being classified as "advanced." If you want to learn more about structures, there is a built-in demo in MATLAB that can be run through the `strucdem` function.

Back to the topic at hand, this block of code can dynamically load data based on the contents of the current folder, without needing any adjustments if the exact number of participants or files changes, files are renamed, or any numbers are skipped.

```
1 dirlist = dir('subject4*');
2
3 for i = 1:length(dirlist)
4     load(dirlist(i).name)
5     nTrial(i) = length(ER);
6 end
7
8 nTrial
```

5.6.4 Time to Automate the Analyses

Let's get started on making this code do the analyses for us by calculating the condition-specific means. First, let's use this version of the code as a starting point. This code is also saved as **analysis1.m** in the current folder.

```
1 lastsub = 5;
2 skipped = [ ];
3
4 sublist = setdiff(1:lastsub,skipped);
5
6 for sub = sublist
7     load(sprintf('subject4%02.0f',sub))
8 end
```

Next, let's just paste in some of the analyses we did earlier, but add in semicolons so that the output doesn't get printed to the command window every time. Let's also add in some comments, so our code is easier for us to read later on. This version of the code is also saved as **analysis2.m**.

```
1 % only load the data for a few subjects for now
2 lastsub = 5;
3 skipped = [ ];
4
5 sublist = setdiff(1:lastsub,skipped);
6
7 for sub = sublist
8
9     %load the .mat life
10    load(sprintf('subject4%02.0f',sub))
11
12    % calculate the subject's mean error rates
13    ERsub(1) = mean(ER(find(D==.5 & Dpen==0)));
14    ERsub(2) = mean(ER(find(D==1 & Dpen==0)));
15    ERsub(3) = mean(ER(find(D==2 & Dpen==0)));
16    ERsub(4) = mean(ER(find(D==.5 & Dpen==1.5)));
17
18    % response times too
19    RTsub(1) = mean(RT(find(D==.5 & Dpen==0)));
20    RTsub(2) = mean(RT(find(D==1 & Dpen==0)));
21    RTsub(3) = mean(RT(find(D==2 & Dpen==0)));
22    RTsub(4) = mean(RT(find(D==.5 & Dpen==1.5)));
23
24    % print this is is to the screen for now
25    sub
26    ERsub
27    RTsub
28 end
```

When you run this script, you should get the following output:

```
 1 sub =
 2        1
 3 ERsub =
 4      0.2882      0.2092      0.2020      0.2794
 5 RTsub =
 6      0.6940      0.7432      0.8165      0.7651
 7 sub =
 8        2
 9 ERsub =
10      0.1809      0.1264      0.0677      0.1294
11 RTsub =
12      0.5099      0.5011      0.5770      0.5277
13 sub =
14        3
15 ERsub =
16      0.1510      0.1957      0.1577      0.2186
17 RTsub =
18      0.8935      0.8119      1.0018      0.8639
19 sub =
20        4
21 ERsub =
22      0.1677      0.1752      0.1000      0.1075
23 RTsub =
24      0.7670      0.7788      0.7942      0.6999
25 sub =
26        5
27 ERsub =
28           0      0.0236           0      0.0065
29 RTsub =
30      0.7652      0.9697      0.9011      0.8451
```

Great! Now we can get the error rates and response times for each of these five participants. However, every time the `for` loop cycles, the contents of ERsub and RTsub are overwritten. While it was important to write the code this way first, the script is not yet able to store the means for each participant.

5.6.5 Combining Variables in a for Loop

Combining variables through concatenation

One way to combine the variables is to concatenate their values. The simplest ways to do this are `horzcat` and `vertcat`. Let's do a quick example.

```
1 >> ERsub1 = [ 0.2882      0.2092      0.2020      0.2794 ];
2 >> ERsub2 = [ 0.1809      0.1264      0.0677      0.1294 ];
3 >> horzcat(ERsub1,ERsub2)
4 ans =
5    Columns 1 through 5
6      0.2882    0.2092    0.2020    0.2794    0.1809
7    Columns 6 through 8
8      0.1264    0.0677    0.1294
9 >> vertcat(ERsub1,ERsub2)
10 ans =
11      0.2882    0.2092    0.2020    0.2794
12      0.1809    0.1264    0.0677    0.1294
```

There is also **cat**, which is more general-purpose. **cat** takes three inputs: first, the dimension you want to concatenate across, followed by the two to-be-concatenated variables.

```
1 >> cat(1,ERsub1,ERsub2)
2 ans =
3      0.2882    0.2092    0.2020    0.2794
4      0.1809    0.1264    0.0677    0.1294
5 >> cat(2,ERsub1,ERsub2)
6 ans =
7    Columns 1 through 5
8      0.2882    0.2092    0.2020    0.2794    0.1809
9    Columns 6 through 8
10      0.1264    0.0677    0.1294
```

Basically, **cat** can do everything that **horzcat** and **vertcat** can do, but is more flexible.

As shown in Chapter 1, we also can concatenate variables without using any functions directly but instead by just using the square brackets.

```
1 >> [ERsub1 ERsub2]
2 ans =
3    Columns 1 through 5
4      0.2882    0.2092    0.2020    0.2794    0.1809
5    Columns 6 through 8
6      0.1264    0.0677    0.1294
7 >> [ERsub1, ERsub2]
8 ans =
9    Columns 1 through 5
10      0.2882    0.2092    0.2020    0.2794    0.1809
```

(Continued)

(Continued)

```
11   Columns 6 through 8
12      0.1264    0.0677    0.1294
13 >> [ERsub1; ERsub2]
14 ans =
15      0.2882    0.2092    0.2020    0.2794
16      0.1809    0.1264    0.0677    0.1294
```

Let's try these out with our **for** loop, as shown in **analysis3.m**.

```
1 % only load the data for a few subjects for now
2 lastsub = 5;
3 skipped = [ ];
4
5 sublist = setdiff(1:lastsub,skipped);
6
7 % initialize variables for sorting ERs and RTs across participants
8 ERs = [];
9 RTs = [];
10
11 for sub = sublist
12
13     %load the .mat life
14     load(sprintf('subject4%02.of',sub))
15
16     % calculate the subject's mean error rates
17     ERsub(1) = mean(ER(find(D==.5 & Dpen==0)));
18     ERsub(2) = mean(ER(find(D==1 & Dpen==0)));
19     ERsub(3) = mean(ER(find(D==2 & Dpen==0)));
20     ERsub(4) = mean(ER(find(D==.5 & Dpen==1.5)));
21
22     % response times too
23     RTsub(1) = mean(RT(find(D==.5 & Dpen==0)));
24     RTsub(2) = mean(RT(find(D==1 & Dpen==0)));
25     RTsub(3) = mean(RT(find(D==2 & Dpen==0)));
26     RTsub(4) = mean(RT(find(D==.5 & Dpen==1.5)));
27
28     % store these values for later
29         ERs = [ ERs; ERsub ];
30         RTs = [ RTs; RTsub];
31 end
32
33 % let's see what we got
34 ERs
35 RTs
```

And the output is as follows:

```
 1 ERs =
 2       0.2882      0.2092      0.2020      0.2794
 3       0.1809      0.1264      0.0677      0.1294
 4       0.1510      0.1957      0.1577      0.2186
 5       0.1677      0.1752      0.1000      0.1075
 6            0      0.0236           0      0.0065
 7 RTs =
 8       0.6940      0.7432      0.8165      0.7651
 9       0.5099      0.5011      0.5770      0.5277
10       0.8935      0.8119      1.0018      0.8639
11       0.7670      0.7788      0.7942      0.6999
12       0.7652      0.9697      0.9011      0.8451
```

Let's try skipping over participant 4 again. Here, we would get a bit of a different output.

```
 1 ERs =
 2       0.2882      0.2092      0.2020      0.2794
 3       0.1809      0.1264      0.0677      0.1294
 4       0.1510      0.1957      0.1577      0.2186
 5            0      0.0236           0      0.0065
 6 RTs =
 7       0.6940      0.7432      0.8165      0.7651
 8       0.5099      0.5011      0.5770      0.5277
 9       0.8935      0.8119      1.0018      0.8639
10       0.7652      0.9697      0.9011      0.8451
```

Notice that no line was left for the fourth participant? There are no NaNs or zeros or anything else. In this case, we can just use mean normally, but cannot use sublist as it is not needed and will instead return an error.

```
1 >> mean(ERs)
2 ans =
3     0.1550      0.1387      0.1069      0.1585
4 >> mean(ERs(sublist,:))
5 ??? Index exceeds matrix dimensions.
```

This error is because the sublist variable asks MATLAB to access the fifth row of ERs, which does not exist. We will discuss errors in more detail in Chapter 6.

There are other ways we could also have done this, rather than using concatenation.

Initializing a matrix first for easy storage

Another way to solve this problem is to make an initial matrix with one of the functions we learned earlier, and then substitute in the means for that particular participant. Let's do this now.

```
1  % only load the data for a few subjects for now
2  lastsub = 5;
3  skipped = [ ];
4
5  sublist = setdiff(1:lastsub,skipped);
6
7  % initialize variables for storing ERs and RTs across participants
8  ERs = nan(length(sublist),4);
9  RTs = nan(length(sublist),4);
10
11 for sub = sublist
12
13     % load the .mat life
14     load(sprintf('subject4%02.0f', sub))
15
16     % calculate the subject's mean error rates
17     ERsub(1) = mean(ER(find(D==.5 & Dpen==0)));
18     ERsub(2) = mean(ER(find(D==1 & Dpen==0)));
19     ERsub(3) = mean(ER(find(D==2 & Dpen==0)));
20     ERsub(4) = mean(ER(find(D==.5 & Dpen==1.5)));
21
22     % response times too
23     RTsub(1) = mean(RT(find(D==.5 & Dpen==0)));
24     RTsub(2) = mean(RT(find(D==1 & Dpen==0)));
25     RTsub(3) = mean(RT(find(D==2 & Dpen==0)));
26     RTsub(4) = mean(RT(find(D==.5 & Dpen==1.5)));
27
28     % store these values for later
29     ERs(sub,:) = ERsub;
30     RTs(sub,:) = RTsub;
31 end
32
33 % let's see what we got
34 ERs
35 RTs
```

The output here looks identical to when we used concatenation.

```
 1 ERs =
 2       0.2882        0.2092        0.2020        0.2794
 3       0.1809        0.1264        0.0677        0.1294
 4       0.1510        0.1957        0.1577        0.2186
 5       0.1677        0.1752        0.1000        0.1075
 6            0        0.0236             0        0.0065
 7 RTs =
 8       0.6940        0.7432        0.8165        0.7651
 9       0.5099        0.5011        0.5770        0.5277
10       0.8935        0.8119        1.0018        0.8639
11       0.7670        0.7788        0.7942        0.6999
12       0.7652        0.9697        0.9011        0.8451
```

Here I used nan, so it's easy to tell if some data are missing. This code is saved as **analysis4.m** in the current folder.

If we try to skip participant number 4, let's see how the **ERs** and **RTs** variables would look then.

```
 1 ERs =
 2       0.2882        0.2092        0.2020        0.2794
 3       0.1809        0.1264        0.0677        0.1294
 4       0.1510        0.1957        0.1577        0.2186
 5          NaN           NaN           NaN           NaN
 6            0        0.0236             0        0.0065
 7 RTs =
 8       0.6940        0.7432        0.8165        0.7651
 9       0.5099        0.5011        0.5770        0.5277
10       0.8935        0.8119        1.0018        0.8639
11          NaN           NaN           NaN           NaN
12       0.7652        0.9697        0.9011        0.8451
```

If we then looked at the means we would need to either use our **sublist** variable to select the rows to average with or use nanmean. Here, we don't have to worry as much about accidentally averaging in zero values, as mean would simply return NaNs, rather than returning incorrect mean values.

```
 1 >> mean(ERs)
 2 ans =
 3     NaN    NaN    NaN    NaN
 4 >> mean(ERs(sublist,:))
 5 ans =
 6     0.1550      0.1387      0.1069      0.1585
 7 >> nanmean(ERs)
 8 ans =
 9     0.1550      0.1387      0.1069      0.1585
```

We could also use the `isnan` function we discussed previously, though this implementation is a bit more work. Here, I'll show you the steps I took myself to implement this alternative solution.

```
 1 >> find(isnan(ERs))
 2 ans =
 3       4
 4       9
 5      14
 6      19
 7 >> isnan(ERs)
 8 ans =
 9       0     0     0     0
10       0     0     0     0
11       0     0     0     0
12       1     1     1     1
13       0     0     0     0
14 >> sum(isnan(ERs))
15 ans =
16       1     1     1     1
17  >> sum(isnan(ERs),2)
18 ans =
19       0
20       0
21       0
22       4
23       0
24 >> sum(isnan(ERs),2)>0
25 ans =
26       0
27       0
28       0
29       1
30       0
31        >>~sum(isnan(ERs),2)>0
32 ans =
33       1
34       1
35       1
36       0
37       1
38 >> find(~sum(isnan(ERs),2)>0)
39 ans =
40       1
41       2
42       3
43       5
44 >> mean(ERs(find(~sum(isnan(ERs),2)>0),:))
45 ans =
46      0.1550     0.1387     0.1069     0.1585
```

This code can be further refined by writing directly into the ERs and RTs variables, rather than using ERsub and RTsub as intermediates. This is done in analysis5.m and shown below.

```
 1 % only load the data for a few subjects for now
 2 lastsub = 5;
 3 skipped = [ 4 ];
 4
 5 sublist = setdiff(1:lastsub,skipped);
 6
 7 % initalize variables for strong ERs and RTs across participants
 8 ERs = nan(length(sublist),4);
 9 RTs = nan(length(sublist),4);
10
11 for sub = sublist
12
13     % load the .mat file
14     load(sprintf('subject4%20.0f', sub))
15
16     % calculate the subject's mean error rates
17     ERs(sub,1) = mean(ER(find(D==.5 & Dpen==0)));
18     ERs(sub,2) = mean(ER(find(D==1 & Dpen==0)));
19     ERs(sub,3) = mean(ER(find(D==2 & Dpen==0)));
20     ERs(sub,4) = mean(ER(find(D==.5 & Dpen==1.5)));
21
22     % response times too
23     RTs(sub,1) = mean(RT(find(D==.5 & Dpen==0)));
24     RTs(sub,2) = mean(RT(find(D==1 & Dpen==0)));
25     RTs(sub,3) = mean(RT(find(D==2 & Dpen==0)));
26     RTs(sub,4) = mean(RT(find(D==.5 & Dpen==1.5)));
27
28 end
29
30 % let's see what we got
31 ERs
32 RTs
```

The output remains the same as before.

If we try and further increase the efficiency of our code, we can also reduce the repetitive lines where we calculate the error rates and response times by nesting an additional for loop within our existing one, and making our code cycle through the four conditions rather than doing so manually as we did before.

```
1  %% settings
2  lastsub = 5;
3  skipped = [ 4 ];
4
5  condD = [ .5 1 2 .5];
6  condDpen = [ 0 0 0 1.5 ];
7
8  %% analyses start here
9  sublist = setdiff(1:lastsub,skipped);
10
11 % initialize variables for storing ERs and RTs across participants
12 ERs = nan(length(sublist),4);
13 RTs = nan(length(sublist),4);
14
15 for sub = sublist
16
17     % load the .mat file
18     load(sprintf('subject4%02.0f',sub))
19
20     % calculate the subject's means
21     for cond = 1:length(condD)
22         ERs(sub,cond) = mean(ER(find(D==condD(cond) & ...
23             Dpen==condDpen(cond))));
24         RTs(sub,cond) = mean(RT(find(D==condD(cond) & ...
25             Dpen==condDpen(cond))));
26     end
27
28 end
29
30 % let's see what we got
31 ERs
32 RTs
```

See how the code is a bit cleaner now? It looks a bit more complicated as well, but I'm sure you can handle it by this point.

★ **TIP #35**

If our analysis was a bit more complicated with additional variables, we might even want to make a loop to automate the same line of code for the ERs, RTs, and our other additional variables. This could be done through the use of the `eval` function. This function can *evaluate* a string and run it as a command. Give this a try with eval (`'1+1'`) and eval (`'test=12'`). eval can be a powerful function, especially if combined with `sprintf`. ∎

5.6.6 Wrapping It Up

We have now successfully used `for` loops to conduct basic analyses on multiple subjects. Let's work on adding some code to calculate the means and SEMs across the sample, making a figure or two and expanding our analysis to the full sample of participants.

```
1 mERs = mean(ERs(sublist,:));
2 semERs = std(ERs(sublist,:))./sqrt(length(sublist));
3 mRTs = mean(RTs(sublist,:));
4 semRTs = std(RTs(sublist,:))./sqrt(length(sublist));
```

And now let's plot the results.

```
1 xticks = {'.5','1','2','.5+1.5'};
2 subplot(2,1,1)
3 bar(mERs,'facecolor',[ .6 .6 .8 ])
4 hold on
5 errorbar(1:4,mERs,semERs,'.k','markersize',1)
6 xlabel('Delay Condition')
7 ylabel('Error Rate')
8 axis([ .5 4.5 0 .3 ])
9 set(gca,'XTick',1:4)
10 set(gca,'YTick',0:.05:.3)
11 set(gca,'XTickLabel',xticks)
12 set(gca,'TickDir','out')
13 box off
14 hold off
15
16 subplot(2,1,2)
17 bar(mRTs,'facecolor',[ .6 .6 .8 ])
18 hold on
19 errorbar(1:4,mRTs,semRTs,'.k','markersize',1)
20 xlabel('Delay Condition')
21 ylabel('Reaction Time (s)')
22 axis([ .5 4.5 .6 1 ])
23 plot([0 5],[.6 .6],'k')
24 set(gca,'XTick',1:4)
25 set(gca,'YTick',.6:.1:1)
26 set(gca,'XTickLabel',xticks)
27 set(gca,'TickDir','out')
28 box off
29 hold off
```

The result of this code is shown in Figure 5.2

Figure 5.2　Error rates and reaction times for the first five participants.

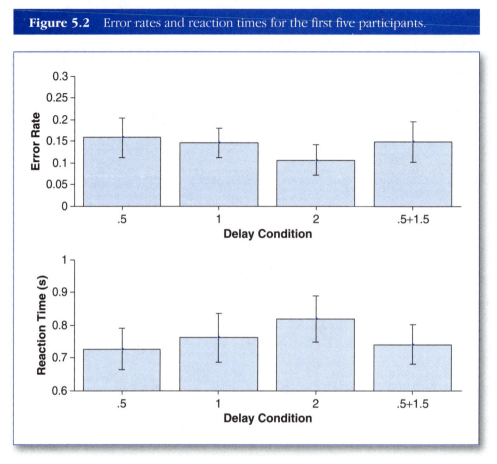

If we adjust lastsub so that we load the full sample of 20 participants, our resulting figure will look like Figure 5.3 on page 124. The code for this version of the script is as follows and is also saved as **analysis7.m**.

```
1 %% settings
2 lastsub = 20;
3 skipped = [ ];
4
5 condD = [ .5 1 2 .5];
6 condDpen = [ 0 0 0 1.5 ];
7
8 %% analyses start here
9 sublist = setdiff(1:lastsub,skipped);
10
11 % initialize variables for strong ERs and RTs across participants
12 ERs = nan(length(sublist),4);
```

```
13 RTs = nan(length(sublist),4);
14
15 for sub = sublist
16
17     %load the .mat file
18     load(sprintf('subject4%02.0f',sub))
19
20     % calculate the subject's means
21     for cond = 1:length(condD)
22         ERs(sub,cond) = mean(ER(find(D==condD(cond) & ...
23                 Dpen==condDpen(cond))));
24         RTs(sub,cond) = mean(RT(find(D==condD(cond) & ...
25                 Dpen==condDpen(cond))));
26     end
27
28 end
29
30 % states on the sample
31 mERs = mean(ERs(sublist,:));
32 semERs = std(ERs(sublist,:))./sqrt(length(sublist));
33 mRTs = mean(RTs(sublist,:));
34 semRTs = std(RTs(sublist,:))./sqrt(length(sublist));
35
36 %% figure
37 xticks ={'.5','1','2','.5+1.5'};
38 subplot(2,1,1)
39 bar(mERs,'facecolor',[ .6 .6 .8 ])
40 hold on
41 errorbar(1:4,mERs,semERs,'.k','markersize',1)
42 xlabel('Delay Condition')
43 ylabel('Error Rate')
44 axis([ .5 4.5 0 .3 ])
45 set(gca,'XTick',1:4)
46 set(gca,'YTick',0:.05:.3)
47 set(gca,'XTickLabel',xticks)
48 set(gca,'TickDir','out')
49 box off
50 hold off
51
52 subplot(2,1,2)
53 bar(mRTs,'facecolor',[ .6 .6 .8 ])
54 hold on
55 errorbar(1:4,mRTs,semRTs,'.k','markersize',1)
56 xlabel('Delay Condition')
57 ylabel('Reaction Time (s)')
```

(Continued)

(Continued)

```
58 axis([ .5 4.5 .6 1 ])
59 plot([0 5],[.6 .6],'k')
60 set(gca,'XTick',1:4)
61 set(gca,'YTick',.6:.1:1)
62 set(gca,'XTickLabel',xticks)
63 set(gca,'TickDir','out')
64 box off
65 hold off
```

Figure 5.3　Error rates and reaction times for all 20 participants.

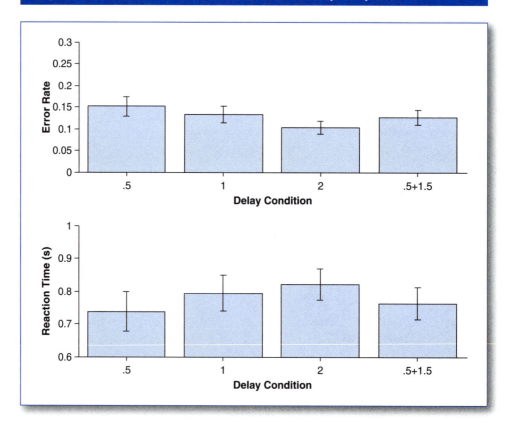

5.7 Making Our Scripts Interactive

Scripts are great in that they can automatically run many lines of code for us, but sometimes we still need some degree of interaction with the code as it runs.

Let's start with a simple script, to get us started.

```
1 lastsub = 10;
2
3 for sub = 1:lastsub
4       sub
5       %load files and do analysis
6 end
```

As you can see, this script is only designed to represent a skeleton of what we were using previously. This script can be found in the **demo** folder, named as **interact1.m**.

If we try and run it, all it does is count the for loop cycles.

```
 1 >> interact1
 2 sub =
 3        1
 4 sub =
 5        2
 6 sub =
 7        3
 8 sub =
 9        4
10 sub =
11        5
12 sub =
13        6
14 sub =
15        7
16 sub =
17        8
18 sub =
19        9
20 sub =
21       10
```

Currently, the only variable we would adjust in this script itself is **lastsub**. What if we could manually edit this value, without editing the script itself? I hope you're not surprised to hear that MATLAB has a function for that! The **input** function does exactly this. If we replace the first line of our program with the line below, MATLAB will prompt us for the value of lastsub when we run the script, thus adjusting the number of times the **for** loop gets run.

```
1 lastsub = input('What was the last subject number? ');
```

This edited file has already been saved as `interact2.m`. Let's run it and specify 5 as the value.

```
 1 >> interact2
 2 What was the last subject number? 5
 3 sub =
 4      1
 5 sub =
 6      2
 7 sub =
 8      3
 9 sub =
10      4
11 sub =
12      5
```

Great! Now, we can adjust our scripts without editing the `.m` files themselves.

The fact that our script prints out the value of **sub** on every cycle of the loop is a bit clumsy. What if we could have it print a line of text to the MATLAB command window to update it on its progress, without just printing the value of the variable itself? For example, what if we could make it tell us in a sentence that it's now analyzing the data for subject *X*, and what percent done it is. If we have short scripts, this may be a bit excessive, but when our scripts get more complicated and take several minutes to run, the status updates can be quite helpful. They are particularly useful if we think our script may be getting stuck and needs debugging.

Let's do this one in reverse order. The output from our revised script is shown below.

```
 1 >> interact3
 2 What was the last subject number? 8
 3 Processing data from participant 1. 0 percent complete...
 4 Processing data from participant 2. 12 percent complete...
 5 Processing data from participant 3. 25 percent complete...
 6 Processing data from participant 4. 38 percent complete...
 7 Processing data from participant 5. 50 percent complete...
 8 Processing data from participant 6. 62 percent complete...
 9 Processing data from participant 7. 75 percent complete...
10 Processing data from participant 8. 88 percent complete...
11 All done! 100 percent complete.
12 >> interact3
13 What was the last subject number? 3
```

```
14 Processing data from participant 1. 0 percent complete...
15 Processing data from participant 2. 33 percent complete...
16 Processing data from participant 3. 67 percent complete...
17 All done! 100 percent complete.
```

The script that generated this is called `interact3.m` and is shown below.

```
1 lastsub = input('What was the last subject number? ');
2
3 for sub = 1:lastsub
4     disp(sprintf('Processing data from participant %.0f. %.0f Percent
5         complete...',sub,(sub-1)/lastsub*100))
6     % load files and do analysis
7 end
8 disp('All done! 100 percent complete.')
```

Note: Line 4 is broken across both lines 4 and 5 here but not in the script's `.m` file. This was done only because the line was too long to fit on the printed page here.

★ **TIP #36**

If you thought this was useful, you may want to also look into `waitbar`. ■

As you can see, our addition here is the function `disp`, which can be used to print text to the MATLAB command window. While this is nothing special in itself, when combined with `sprintf`, we can make our script provide status updates as it runs.

`disp`, along with `sprintf`, can also do some other useful things, such as this:

```
1 >> date
2 ans =
3 06-Jan-2013
4 >> disp(sprintf('Today is %s.',date))
5 Today is 06-Jan-2013.
```

When your scripts become more complicated, it may also be desirable to divide them into multiple scripts and then have one "main" script that calls the others as needed. As an example, you could have a script that looks like this:

```
1 config
2 loadData
3 doAnalysis
4 mkFigs
```

In this example, `config`, `loadData`, `doAnalysis`, and `mkFigs` are each their own script.

5.8 Building Functions

When you really want to automate a series of commands that you will perform often, you should make a function. Just as MATLAB has many built-in functions that we have been learning to use throughout this book, you can also make your own functions.

When I start making a new function, I usually first start by making a script and working in the command window, and then adjust it to be a function. Let's try making a function equivalent to nanmean, but we'll just call it nmean so it doesn't conflict with MATLAB's own version. First, we need a matrix of some numbers that includes NaNs.

```
1 data = rand(5,4);
2 data(2,2) = NaN;
3 data
```

For me, the output of this code was as follows, though the values are randomly generated based on rand. This code is also saved as **nmean1.m** in the **demo** folder.

```
1 data =
2     0.6557    0.7577    0.7060    0.8235
3     0.0357       NaN    0.0318    0.6948
4     0.8491    0.3922    0.2769    0.3171
5     0.9340    0.6555    0.0462    0.9502
6     0.6787    0.1712    0.0971    0.0344
```

Before we begin, let's confirm that mean won't work and that nanmean does. We will also try doing the averaging both collapsing across the columns and collapsing across rows.

```
 1 >> mean(data)
 2 ans =
 3      0.6307           NaN      0.2316        0.5640
 4 >> mean(data,2)
 5 ans =
 6      0.7357
 7         NaN
 8      0.4588
 9      0.6465
10      0.2454
11 >> nanmean(data)
12 ans =
13      0.6307        0.4942      0.2316        0.5640
14 >> nanmean(data,2)
15 ans =
16      0.7357
17      0.2541
18      0.4588
19      0.6465
20      0.2454
```

Since only one value is a NaN, not a whole row or column, we can't simply skip over that row or column as we did before. Let's use a `for` loop to get the mean for each row and column individually.

To get around the NaN, let's replace it with zero and then use `sum`. We can then divide by the number of non-NaNs to get the 'nanmean'. Let's start with writing the code for this particular NaN value.

```
 1 >> i = 2;
 2 >> data(:,i)
 3 ans =
 4      0.7577
 5         NaN
 6      0.3922
 7      0.6555
 8      0.1712
 9 >> isnan(data(:,i))
10 ans =
11      0
12      1
13      0
14      0
15      0
```

(Continued)

(Continued)

```
16 >> find(isnan(data(:,i)))
17 ans =
18        2
19 >> data0 = data(:,i);
20 >> data0(isnan(data(:,i))) = 0;
21 >> data0
22 data0 =
23        0.7577
24             0
25        0.3922
26        0.6555
27        0.1712
28 >> sum(data0)
29 ans =
30        1.9766
31 >> sum(~isnan(data(:,i)))
32 ans =
33        4
34 >> sum(data0)/sum(~isnan(data(:,i)))
35 ans =
36        0.4942
37 >> nanmean(data(:,i))
38 ans =
39        0.4942
```

And now we can adjust this code to work for the full matrix.

```
 1 >> data
 2 data =
 3        0.6557        0.7577        0.7060        0.8235
 4        0.0357           NaN        0.0318        0.6948
 5        0.8491        0.3922        0.2769        0.3171
 6        0.9340        0.6555        0.0462        0.9502
 7        0.6787        0.1712        0.0971        0.0344
 8 >> isnan(data)
 9 ans =
10        0     0     0     0
11        0     1     0     0
12        0     0     0     0
13        0     0     0     0
14        0     0     0     0
15 >> notnan = sum(~isnan(data))
16 notnan =
17        5     4     5     5
18 >> data0 = data;
```

```
19 >> data0(isnan(data)) = 0;
20 >> data0
21 data0 =
22      0.6557      0.7577      0.7060      0.8235
23      0.0357           0      0.0318      0.6948
24      0.8491      0.3922      0.2769      0.3171
25      0.9340      0.6555      0.0462      0.9502
26      0.6787      0.1712      0.0971      0.0344
27 >> sum(data0)./notnan
28 ans =
29      0.6307      0.4942      0.2316      0.5640
30 >> nanmean(data)
31 ans =
32      0.6307      0.4942      0.2316      0.5640
```

Great! Now, we can isolate the key lines of code and store those in our script.

```
1 data = rand(5,4);
2 data(2,2) = NaN;
3 data
4
5 % count the non-NaNs
6 nontan= sum(~isnan(data));
7
8 % replace the NaN with a zero
9 data0 = data;
10 data0(isnan(data)) = 0;
11
12 nm = sum(data0)./notnan
```

This version of the code is saved as **nmean2.m**. Now, let's make some changes so that we can specify which dimension to average across, such that we can average across the columns instead.

```
1 data = rand(5,4);
2 data(2,2) = NaN;
3 data
4
5 dim = 1;
6
7 % count the non-NaNs
8 notnan = sum(~isnan(data),dim);
```

(Continued)

(Continued)

```
 9
10 % replace the NaN with a zero
11 data0 = data;
12 data0(isnan(data)) = 0;
13
14 nm = sum(data0,dim)./notnan
```

Now, when `dim=1`, the code works as before:

```
1 nm =
2     0.6307     0.4942     0.2316     0.5640
```

When we instead set `dim=2`, we can average across the other dimension.

```
1 nm =
2     0.7357
3     0.2541
4     0.4588
5     0.6465
6     0.2454
```

If we compare this again with **nanmean**, it looks like we have this working perfectly! This version of the script is saved as **nmean3.m**

```
1 >> nanmean(data,2)
2 ans =
3     0.7357
4     0.2541
5     0.4588
6     0.6465
7     0.2454
```

To make a script into a function, we need to add one line at the top, defining it as a function and specifying which variable(s) go in, and which are returned out. The basics of how this works are as follows:

```
1 function out = functionName(in)
```

In our current case, we would want to use the following:

```
1 function nm = nmean4(data,dim)
```

And then we can remove the code that generates the data and dim variables from our new function with **function**. The complete function code is shown below and is named **nmean4.m**.

```
 1 function nm = nmean4(data,dim)
 2
 3 % count the non-NaNs
 4 notnan = sum(~isnan(data),dim);
 5
 6 % replace the NaN wth a zero
 7 data0 = data;
 8 data0(isnan(data)) = 0;
 9
10 nm = sum(data0,dim)./notnan;
```

Let's try it out!

```
 1 >> nmean4(data,1)
 2 ans =
 3      0.6307      0.4942      0.2316      0.5640
 4 >> nmean4(data,2)
 5 ans =
 6      0.7357
 7      0.2541
 8      0.4588
 9      0.6465
10      0.2454
```

Of course, there are always ways to improve our code. For instance, if we don't specify a second input variable (i.e., dim), our function will return an error, while the true nanmean function defaults to the first dimension.

```
 1 >> nmean4(data)
 2 ??? Input argument "dim" is undefined.
 3 Error in ==> nmean4 at 4
 4 notnan = sum(~isnan(data),dim);
 5
 6 >> nanmean(data)
 7 ans =
 8      0.6307      0.4942      0.2316      0.5640
```

This would be a good instance to use an if statement with the exist function. exist returns a 1 or a 0, based on if a specified variable exists. Here, we could use something like this:

```
1 if ~exist('dim')
2     dim = 1;
3 end
```

These lines were added to **nmean5.m**.

```
1 >> nmean5(data)
2 ans =
3     0.6307     0.4942     0.2316     0.5640
```

One more useful addition would be if we could also return the **notnan** to the user, if they want it. Functions by design do not share the same variable space as our workspace. Thus, any variable created in a function is not available to us outside the function, unless we explicitly have it returned by the function. For instance, we currently can't access the variable **notnan**.

```
1 >> notnan
2 ??? Undefined function or variable 'notnan'.
```

To have this variable also returned from our function, we need to adjust the first line of our function:

```
1 function [nm,notnan] = nmean6(data,dim)
```

When we use **nmean6**, it generally will function the same as **nmean5**. However, if we specify the variables for its output to be stored in, we can also get the **notnan** data.

```
1 >> nmean6(data)
2 ans =
3     0.6307     0.4942     0.2316     0.5640
4 >> v1 = nmean6(data)
5 v1 =
6     0.6307     0.4942     0.2316     0.5640
7 >> [v1,v2] = nmean6(data)
8 v1 =
9     0.6307     0.4942     0.2316     0.5640
10 v2 =
11        5      4      5      5
12 >> [v1,v2] = nmean6(data,2)
13 v1 =
```

```
14      0.7357
15      0.2541
16      0.4588
17      0.6465
18      0.2454
19 v2  =
20         4
21         3
22         4
23         4
24         4
```

That about wraps this up. Functions can be quite useful for multiline calculations you use repeatedly, especially because they have their own internal workspace that does not affect our own workspace. Test this out yourself using who or whos.

5.9 Toolboxes

Before we end our chapter on automating our analyses, let's talk about toolboxes. Toolboxes are packages of functions that work together and share a common theme. MATLAB itself has a number of toolboxes that are separable from the core installation, such as the Statistics Toolbox. In Chapter 9, we will discuss toolboxes made by The MathWorks Inc., as well as by others, that may be particularly useful for behavioral researchers.

EXERCISES

Now that we can automate our analyses, let's try and improve some of our previous answers, and then take it one step further.

1. Using your new knowledge, calculate the average valence for each word type from the worddb data set. (Repeat of Chapter 3, Question 6)

2. Make a bar graph for the familiarity and personal use ratings. (Repeat of Chapter 4, Question 2)

3. Using the decision1 data set, make a script to test if motion direction influenced error rate.

4. Write a function that will output the number of occurrences (e.g., frequency) of each possible value from an inputted variable. As an example, use the first subject from the `decision1` data set:

```
1 >> load subject401
2 >> freq(blocknum)
3 ans =
4        1     247
5        2     147
6        3     347
7        4     239
8        5     150
```

5. Determine the order of the delay conditions (i.e., what was in each block).

See page 206 for the solutions. I hope you can see why loops and functions can be so useful! Next, we will learn how to debug and optimize our code.

FUNCTION REVIEW

General: `whos`

Scripts and functions: `edit % %{ %}` `echo sprintf eval input disp function`

Conditional statements and loops: `if else elseif end for while`

Matrix operations: `zeros ones rand randn nan repmat horzcat vertcat cat`

6

DEBUG AND OPTIMIZE

Now that you are beginning to be fairly competent in MATLAB, we should talk about what to do when you're making your own code and things aren't going as planned. Errors can be frustrating to all of us, especially those without much previous experience in programming.

6.1 General Practices

In general, save often but also save backups of previous versions of your code (e.g., using revision numbers as done in this book or using last-edited dates). Having previous versions of your scripts and functions saved can go a long way in helping you solve an error, as you can "roll back" parts of your script and potentially easily correct your error and avoid more involved debugging issues.

6.2 Breaking Out of Unresponsive Code

For beginners, one type of error is even more problematic than an actual error in MATLAB being unresponsive because it is still "busy" when it really should have finished running the script or function. The usual cause of this is a bug in a `for` or `while` loop that prevents the loop from ever finishing. One way to prevent this from happening in the first place is to use `disp` to get status updates as your script runs, but this isn't a particularly helpful suggestion when your MATLAB process is already unresponsive.

To have MATLAB abort the current command without killing its process directly (e.g., "End Task," "Force Quit," or "kill"), press CTRL+C. You may have to press this several times if MATLAB was stuck in a nested loop. MATLAB will report an error on the line where it was when it aborted, but this line is usually not related to the actual issue. You can also have MATLAB automatically abort the current script or function if a certain condition is met by using the `break` function in conjunction with an `if` statement. Note that `break` can only abort the innermost loop (see `help` for more details).

6.3 Locating the Error

If you're working on code in the MATLAB command window, usually you can locate your errors fairly easily, even if you don't yet know what is wrong with the code. When working with scripts and functions, this isn't as easy. Though MATLAB will provide you with a line number for where your code is producing an error, sometimes that's not the best place to actually fix the code.

In the case of scripts, the best approach is to use `disp` to get status updates and see which portions of your code are being run and which are not. Another option is to use `pause`, which causes MATLAB to pause the script and wait for you to press a key before it will continue. `echo` is also useful to see what portions of the code are being run. When you get an error, you may also want to use `who` or `whos` to see which variables are in your workspace and what their values are.

With functions, debugging is a bit more difficult, as functions have their own internal workspace that you can't access if the code returns an error or if you use CTRL+C or `break` to abort the code. In this situation, the best function you can use is `keyboard`. This function is great in that it pauses the function where it stands and lets you take over with the *keyboard*. As a result, you can now check the contents of variables that are internal to the function and work to ascertain what is wrong with your code. After you are done, type `return` to have MATLAB continue running the function from where it paused. You can also alternatively type `dbquit` to exit this debug mode and completely abort the current function or code.

6.4 Common Errors: Typing Related

Now that we are better able to localize our problematic lines of code, we need to learn what errors that MATLAB reports really mean and what is the likely cause. Here, we will go through the most common MATLAB errors that you are likely to encounter, along with a simple example that can create them and where to look to remedy them.

Expression or statement is incorrect—possibly unbalanced (, {, or [

This error simply means that the number of brackets you open (of any type, (, [, or {) does not match the number that you close. MATLAB usually tries to point out where in the line the error is, but it may not be correct. This is a particularly common error and arises when you combine many functions within one line of code.

```
1 >> disp(sprintf('Today is %s.',date))
2 Today is 06-Jan-2013.
3 >> disp(sprintf(('Today is %s.',date))
4 ??? disp(sprintf(('Today is %s.',date))
5                  |
6 Error: Expression or statement is incorrect--possibly unbalanced (, {,
7 or [.
```

The simplest solution for this is to take apart the line of code and work back from the inside out and see how much of it works, and confirm that the values returned actually make sense. Below is an example of how this can look.

Too many input arguments

This error message means that you are providing more input variables into a function than it is designed to handle. However, it is more likely that you either made a mistake with the brackets, where you have all the brackets you need (i.e., not an imbalance), but that one or more of them is in the wrong position. It is also possible that you may have accidentally skipped over a step in the logic and missed using one of your functions. Here are examples of either likely mistake.

```
1 >> disp(sprintf('Today is %s.',date))
2 Today is 06-Jan-2013.
3 >> disp(sprintf('Today is %s.'),date)
4 ??? Error using ==> disp
5 Too many input arguments.
6 >> disp('Today is %s.',date)
7 ??? Error using ==> disp
8 Too many input arguments.
```

Undefined function or variable . . .

This error is fairly straightforward: You made a typo, such that the function or variable you are referring to doesn't exist. Since the errors tell you what doesn't exist, it should be easy to search your code for the typo.

```
1 >> disp(sprintf('Today is %s.',date))
2 Today is 06-Jan-2013.
3 >> disp(sprintf('Today is %s.',dat))
4 ??? Undefined function or variable 'dat'.
```

Undefined function or method . . . for input arguments of type . . .

This is almost the same as the previous error, but it occurs when your function has inputs specified.

```
1 >> disp(sprintf('Today is %s.',date))
2 Today is 06-Jan-2013.
3 >> dis(sprintf('Today is %s.',date))
4 ??? Undefined function or method 'dis' for input arguments
5 of type 'char'.
6 >> disp(sprint('Today is %s.',date))
7 ??? Undefined function or method 'sprint' for input arguments
8 of type 'char'.
```

Inner matrix dimensions must agree

This error is usually caused by accidentally telling MATLAB to do matrix multiplication (*) rather than element-wise multiplication (.*). (Also see p. 12.)

```
1 >> ones(2,4) * ones(2,4)
2 ??? Error using ==> mtimes
3 Inner matrix dimensions must agree.
4 >> ones(2,4) .* ones(2,4)
5 ans =
6      1     1     1     1
7      1     1     1     1
```

6.5 Common Errors: Value Related

The previous common errors were all based on some sort of typing error where MATLAB was confused by the bracket placement or was not sure what variable you were referring to. The next set of common errors comprises those related to the contents of your variables and how you are attempting to interact with them.

Index exceeds matrix dimensions

This error occurs when you try to refer to an index that does not exist in the matrix. Specifically, the index you provided was larger than that of the matrix.

In the case of this error, you are likely to have accidentally swapped your indexes for the row and column dimensions. Here, we'll make a quick example matrix, so we can try and reproduce and isolate these errors.

```
 1 >> M = rand(8,4)
 2 M =
 3        0.1656      0.2290      0.1067      0.2599
 4        0.6020      0.9133      0.9619      0.8001
 5        0.2630      0.1524      0.0046      0.4314
 6        0.6541      0.8258      0.7749      0.9106
 7        0.6892      0.5383      0.8173      0.1818
 8        0.7482      0.9961      0.8687      0.2638
 9        0.4505      0.0782      0.0844      0.1455
10        0.0838      0.4427      0.3998      0.1361
11 >> M(3,6)
12 ??? Index exceeds matrix dimensions.
13 >> M(6,3)
14 ans =
15        0.8687
```

Attempted to access . . . index out of bounds because size . . .

This error is very similar to the previous one, but here we are referring to a whole row or column of the matrix rather than a single index.

A likely cause of this error is using `length` when your dimension of interest is *not* the longest. Here you should use `size`. Note that `length` is effectively the same as `max(size)`.

```
1 for i = 1:length(M)
2     meanM(i) = mean(M(:,i));
3 end
4 meanM
```

Using `length` produces the following error:

```
1 ??? Attempted to access M(:,5); index out of bounds because
2 size(M)=[8,4].
```

Using `size`, we can see that we should be using the second dimension.

```
1 >> size(M)
2 ans =
3     8    4
```

The corrected code would look as follows.

```
1 for i = 1:size(M,2)
2     meanM(i) = mean(M(:,i));
3 end
4 meanM
```

As noted earlier, using `size(M,1)` in this particular case would be effectively the same as using `length`, as `length(M)==max(size(M))`.

Subscript indices must either be real positive integers or logicals

This error occurs when you attempt to access an index of a variable that is simply not possible, such as a zero or a non-integer (i.e., a number that has decimals).

```
1 >> M(1)
2 ans =
3     0.1656
4 >> M(0)
5 ??? Subscript indices must either be real positive integers
6 or logicals.
7 >> M(3.4)
8 ??? Subscript indices must either be real positive integers
9 or logicals.
```

In all likelihood, you did not type this yourself and instead fed one variable in as the index for the other. You probably forgot to include the `find` function or maybe `round`.

Subscripted assignment dimension mismatch

This error occurs when you copy values from one matrix to another, but the variables aren't of the same length. The same error is produced regardless of which is longer.

```
1 >> N = nan(4,2);
2 >> N(1,:)
3 ans =
4     NaN NaN
5 >> M(1,:)
6 ans =
7      0.1656    0.2290    0.1067    0.2599
8 >> N(1,:) = M(1,:)
9 ??? Subscripted assignment dimension mismatch.
10 >> M(1,:) = N(1,:)
11 ??? Subscripted assignment dimension mismatch.
12 >> length(N(1,:))
13 ans =
14     2
15 >> length(M(1,:))
16 ans =
17     4
```

This one is a bit harder to fix, as it really depends on what you meant to do. Nonetheless, one possible solution is to only copy the number of values that would fit. Depending on which variable is the longer one, you may need to change the left or the right side of the equal sign. In either case, the key point is to accommodate the shorter of the two variables.

```
1 >> M(1,1:length(N(1,:))) = N(1,:)
2 M =
3        NaN       NaN    0.1067    0.2599
4     0.6020    0.9133    0.9619    0.8001
5     0.2630    0.1524    0.0046    0.4314
6     0.6541    0.8258    0.7749    0.9106
7     0.6892    0.5383    0.8173    0.1818
8     0.7482    0.9961    0.8687    0.2638
9     0.4505    0.0782    0.0844    0.1455
10     0.0838    0.4427    0.3998    0.1361
```

```
1 >> N(1,:) = M(1,1:length(N(1,:)))
2 N =
3     0.1656    0.2290
4        NaN       NaN
5        NaN       NaN
6        NaN       NaN
```

In an assignment A(I) = B, the number of elements in B and I must be the same

This error is quite similar to the last, but this one occurs when you try and store multiple values from one variable into a single index of another variable. This can usually be solved by adjusting your code to store the multiple values of one variable into the same number of values in the second variable, but you should be particularly careful here to make sure that this is what you intended.

```
1 >> A = ones(1,4)
2 A =
3     1    1    1    1
4 >> A(1) = M(1,:)
5 ???  In an assignment   A(I) = B, the number of elements in B
6 and I must be the same.
7 >> A(1,:) = M(1,:)
8 A =
9     0.1656    0.2290    0.1067    0.2599
```

CAT arguments dimensions are not consistent

This error is produced when you try and concatenate two variables that are of different lengths. This error occurs regardless of whether you are using [ ], cat, horzcat, or vertcat.

```
1 >> M(1,:)
2 ans =
3     0.1656    0.2290    0.1067    0.2599
4 >> N(1,:)
5 ans =
6     NaN    NaN
7 >> [ M(1,:) N(1,:) ]
8 ans =
9     0.1656    0.2290    0.1067    0.2599    NaN    NaN
10 >> [ M(1,:); N(1,:) ]
11 ??? Error using ==> vertcat
12 CAT arguments dimensions are not consistent.
```

For this error, it is particularly difficult to suggest how you fix it, as the uses of concatenation can vary greatly. Whatever you do choose, make sure you manually confirm that the resulting output is what you were expecting.

That's all for the common errors. It is quite possible that you will come across other errors as well, but hopefully you will now find the MATLAB error messages a bit less cryptic and you now have a better idea how to resolve them. Good luck!

6.6 Timing Your Code With Tic–Toc

Moving on from debugging, let's work on optimizing your code. In other words, for the sections of Chapter 6 from this point forward, we are assuming that your code works, and you are interested in making it more efficient.

Your first functions toward optimizing your code are `tic` and `toc`. When you use `tic`, MATLAB starts a timer (i.e., a stopwatch). When you use `toc`, MATLAB checks the time elapsed since the last `tic` and outputs it in the command window.

```
1 >> tic
2 >> toc
3 Elapsed time is 2.185080 seconds.
```

You can also use `toc` multiple times to get the time since the most recent `tic`. Using `tic` again will reset to start from zero again.

```
 1 >> tic
 2 >> toc
 3 Elapsed time is 2.185080 seconds.
 4 >> toc
 5 Elapsed time is 7.660244 seconds.
 6 >> tic
 7 >> toc
 8 Elapsed time is 2.335965 seconds.
 9 >> toc
10 Elapsed time is 20.789621 seconds.
11 >> toc
12 Elapsed time is 26.334178 seconds.
```

You can also store the time from `toc` in a variable.

```
1 >> tic
2 >> now = toc
3 now =
4      9.1857
```

You might be wondering: "What's so special about `tic` and `toc`? Why would I care about the time when I'm writing my code?" The answer is to try and optimize your code so that it runs faster. Let's try this out. If you go in the demo folder, you will find a script called `timer1.m`. The contents of this script are copied below. Run this script and see how long it takes to run.

```
1 tic
2
3 numbers = 1:1000;
4 nSum = 0;
5 for i = numbers
6     nSum = nSum + numbers(i);
7 end
8
9 elapsed1 = toc
```

This code is intended to add up all of the numbers from 1 to 1,000. It is intentionally written a bit badly, but hopefully you can still tell that's what it does. Let's run it and see what `elapsed1` is.

```
1 >> timer1
2 elapsed1 =
3      0.0034
```

Now, let's compare this to a much more efficient version of this, which has been saved as `timer2`.

```
1 tic
2
3 numbers = 1:1000;
4 nSum = sum(numbers);
5
6 elapsed2 = toc
```

```
1 >> timer2
2 elapsed2 =
3    3.0986e-05
```

Clearly `elapsed2` is a smaller value. Now, you might be thinking that these aren't very big numbers; does 0.0034 seconds really matter? Well, these are intended to be extremely simple cases, much simpler than your own analyses. It can be very helpful to measure the time it takes for your code to run, especially if you end up doing mathematical simulations, where the same block of code is run tens of thousands of times. Even still, we can also readily see that the small change between `timer1.m` and `timer2.m` made the code run just over 100 times faster.

```
1 >> elapsed1/elapsed2
2 ans =
3    108.2763
```

6.7 Semicolons Are Your Friend

Toward the aim of optimizing your code, one of the smallest changes you can make that will make a world of difference is to add semicolons to the ends of lines that output text to the MATLAB command window. This is especially important if the line of code is contained within a `for` loop. Let's remove a semicolon from `timer1.m`, save the file as `timer3.m`, and see how much difference it makes.

```
 1 >> timer3
 2 nSum =
 3        1
 4 nSum =
 5        3
 6 nSum =
 7        6
 8 nSum =
 9       10
10    ...
11 elapsed3 =
12       0.0213
```

That was a lot slower, but how much?

```
1 >> elapsed3/elapsed1
2 ans =
3      6.3477
4 >> elapsed3/elapsed2
5 ans =
6    687.3026
```

Removing that one character/key press made our script take more than 6 times as long and nearly 700 times as long as our "optimized" version. Clearly, printing to the MATLAB command window can slow scripts down markedly. (Remember that you can use CTRL+C to abort code that takes too long to run!) Suppressing the output can easily speed up your code. This suggestion works well as long as you don't particularly need to be informed of the output of that line of code. If you *do* want to know its contents, such as a counter in a loop that iterates through participant data or some other counter, you can use if in conjunction with mod to get periodic updates on the counter.

mod is a particularly interesting function, but the breadth of its usefulness will probably surprise you. Back in grade school, we learned how to do long division and find the remainder. In analyses, this operation can be quite useful and is more formally known as "modulo." In many programming languages, 'modulo' is abbreviated to 'mod' and uses % as the operator symbol (e.g., 23 % 4 = 3). However, as you know, % is used for other purposes in MATLAB.

One good example of the uses of mod is to determine if a number is odd or even, by dividing it by 2 and seeing what the remainder is.

```
1 >> mod(23,4)
2 ans =
3      3
4 >> mod(23,2)
5 ans =
6      1
7 >> mod(22,2)
8 ans =
9      0
```

Similarly, we can also easily extract the "ones" digit of a number by looking at the remainder after dividing a number by 10.

```
1 >> mod(12,10)
2 ans =
3       2
4 >> mod(113,10)
5 ans =
6       3
7 >> mod(19208,10)
8 ans =
9       8
```

Additionally, mod is quite useful in conjunction with floor.

```
1 >> value = 23;
2 >> divisor = 4;
3 >> mod_value = mod(value,divisor)
4 mod_value =
5       3
6 >> floor_value = floor(value/divisor)
7 floor_value =
8       5
9 >> divisor*floor_value+mod_value
10 ans =
11       23
```

Returning to our current situation with optimizing code, we can use mod in an if statement to only print the contents of a variable periodically, such as every 100th cycle of our for loop, as shown below.

```
1 if mod(i,100) == 0
2     i
3 end
```

We have copied timer1.m, added in this code, and saved it as timer4.m.

```
1 tic
2
3 numbers = 1:1000;
4 nSum = 0;
5 for i = numbers
6     nSum = nSum + numbers(i);
7     if mod(i,100) == 0
8         i
9     end
10 end
11
12 elapsed4 = toc
```

Let's run it and see how it compares.

```
 1 >> timer4
 2 i =
 3     100
 4 i =
 5     200
 6 i =
 7     300
 8 i =
 9     400
10 i =
11     500
12 i =
13     600
14 i =
15     700
16 i =
17     800
18 i =
19     900
20 i =
21             1000
22 elapsed4 =
23       0.0132
```

```
1 >> elapsed4/elapsed1
2 ans =
3     3.9286
4 >> elapsed4/elapsed3
5 ans =
6     0.6189
```

This version is definitely slower than `timer1.m` but not as bad as `timer3.m`. Keep in mind that there is also a cost to adding this additional code for the `if` and `mod`, as MATLAB has to do more calculations on every cycle of the `for` loop. To make this more apparent, let's set the `mod` function to divide by 1, effectively making the code in the `if` statement always run. This file is saved as `timer5.m`.

```
1 >> timer5
2 i =
3     1
4 i =
```

```
 5        2
 6 i =
 7        3
 8 i =
 9        4
10 i =
11        5
12        ...
13 elapsed5 =
14        0.0483
```

```
1 >> elapsed5/elapsed1
2 ans =
3     14.3882
4 >> elapsed5/elapsed4
5 ans =
6      3.6624
7 >> elapsed5/elapsed3
8 ans =
9      2.2667
```

Clearly, this made the script run much slower. That about covers it for `tic` and `toc,` but hopefully, that gave you some idea that even though there are many ways to code an analysis in MATLAB, they are not all equally optimal. That being said, it may sometimes also be better in the long run to make your code more flexible so that it can be reused in a different analysis, despite making the code a bit slower to run.

6.8 Profiling Your Code

If `tic` and `toc` aren't enough for you, MATLAB does have more powerful tools to help you optimize your code. Just like the FBI profilers you see on TV profile unsavory people to better understand what makes them tick, you can use the `profile` function to profile your MATLAB code to better understand what makes your code work. This is the function that you need to clean up complex, resource-hungry MATLAB code. You can find the bottlenecks by profiling your code. A screenshot of the `profile` viewer is shown in Figure 6.1.

Figure 6.1.   Screenshot of the `profile` viewer.

Profile Summary
Generated 09–Jan–2013 23:57:46 using cpu time.

Function Name	Calls	Total Time	Self Time*	Total Time Plot (dark band = self time)
workspacefunc	4	1.264 s	0.211 s	
workspacefunc>getShortValueObjectJ	10	0.632 s	0.421 s	
workspacefunc>getShortValueObjectsJ	1	0.632 s	0.000 s	
timer1	1	0.421 s	0.421 s	
workspacefunc>getStatObjectJ	20	0.421 s	0.000 s	
workspacefunc>getStatObjectM	20	0.421 s	0.211 s	
workspacefunc>getStatObjectsJ	2	0.421 s	0.000 s	
workspacefunc>createComplexScalar	29	0.211 s	0.211 s	
workspacefunc>num2complex	30	0.211 s	0.000 s	
workspacefunc>local_min	10	0.211 s	0.211 s	
workspacefunc>getWhosInformation	1	0 s	0.000 s	
...s.mlwidgets.workspace.WhosInformation (Java method)	1	0 s	0.000 s	

When you are ready to start profiling, just type `profile on`. When you're all done and ready to see the report, type `profile viewer`.

```
1 >> profile on
2 >> % run your code/script here
3 >> profile viewer
```

6.9 A Fresh Pair of Eyes

As a final note, when you're not sure how to solve an error or could use some direction in optimizing your code, don't be afraid to ask a friend to take a look. Hopefully, you know someone else working through this book or who already knows MATLAB. A fresh pair of eyes looking through your code can make all the difference. You sometimes need to ask someone else to proofread a paper you write; your code is no different.

EXERCISES

This time will be a bit different; here we will fix errors and optimize code.

1. Load the **worddb** data set.

   Find the error produced by each line of code, and try and correct the mistake.

2. Code:

```
1 scatter(worddata{10},worddata{8}(1:460))
```

3. Code:

```
1 imagTab = mean(worddata{20}(find(strcmp,worddata{2},'taboo')))
```

4. Code:

```
1 types=unique(worddata(2,1:460))
```

5. Try to optimize this script:

```
1 % find numbers divisible by 3 within certain range
2 numbers = 277:300;
3 div3 = [];
4
5 for n = numbers
6     if (n/3) == round(n/3)
7         div3 = [ div3 n ];
8     end
9 end
10
11 div3
```

Output:

```
1 div3 =
2    279   282   285   288   291   294   297   300
```

See page 209 for the solutions. Next, we will add basic statistics to our MATLAB skills.

FUNCTION REVIEW

General: `mod`

Debug: `break pause keyboard return dbquit`

Timing: `tic toc profile`

7

ELEMENTARY STATISTICS

Thus far, we have learned to do almost everything we need to in MATLAB. However, one major aspect still remains: inferential statistics. Before we can conclude if our experimental manipulation made a difference in the dependent measure, we must test for this difference statistically.

7.1 Confidence Intervals

Calculating a confidence interval is easy, given that you have already determined the standard error of the mean (SEM) and that the data follow a normal distribution. Let's load up the data from the `decision1` data set to try this out. Run the `analysis7.m` script from earlier.

```
1 >> analysis7
```

Usually, we want to calculate the 95% confidence interval (two-tailed), which corresponds to 1.96 standard deviations and would represent the interval of 2.5 to 97.5 percentiles. SEM corresponds to 1 standard deviation of the data and to a 68.2% confidence interval (see Figure 7.1).

We have previously calculated the SEM. To get the interval itself, we need to subtract the SEM from the mean to get the lower bound and add it to the mean. Let's do this for all four of the experiments' conditions.

```
1 >> [ mERs-semERs; mERs+semERs ]
2 ans =
3     0.1289    0.1140    0.0873    0.1089
4     0.1732    0.1517    0.1185    0.1434
```

Figure 7.1 Normal distribution with confidence intervals and percentiles marked.

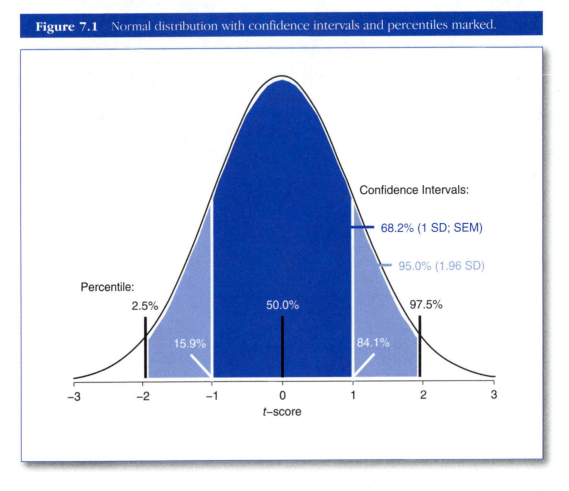

If we want to instead get the 95% confidence intervals, we simply need to multiply the SEM (here, semERs) by 1.96.

```
1 >> [ mERs-semERs*1.96; mERs+semERs*1.96 ]
2 ans =
3     0.1077    0.0960    0.0723    0.0924
4     0.1944    0.1698    0.1335    0.1599
```

7.2 One-Sample and Pairwise-Comparison *t* tests

To directly test if performance is different from a set value or between conditions, we need to do *t* tests. For now, let's take the first condition.

```
1 >> mERs(1)
2 ans =
3     0.1511
```

Is the error rate here significantly different from 0.10? What about 0.15? To answer this, we need to use the `ttest` function. This function can give us several outputs:

```
1 >> help ttest
2  TTEST One-sample and paired-sample t-test.
3     H = TTEST(X) performs a t-test of the hypothesis that the data
4     in the vector X come from a distribution with mean zero, and
5     returns the result of the test in H. H=0 indicates that the null
6     hypothesis ("mean is zero") cannot be rejected at the 5%
7     significance level. H=1 indicates that the null hypothesis can
8     be rejected at the 5% level. The data are assumed to come
9     from a normal distribution with unknown variance.
10
11     ...
12
13     TTEST treats NaNs as missing values, and ignores them.
14
15     H = TTEST(X,M) performs a t-test of the hypothesis that the
16     data in X come from a distribution with mean M. M must be a
17     scalar.
18
19     H = TTEST(X,Y) performs a paired t-test of the hypothesis that
20     two matched samples, in the vectors X and Y, come from
21     distributions with equal means. The difference X-Y is assumed to
22     come from a normal distribution with unknown variance. X and Y
23     must have the same length. X and Y can also be matrices or N-D
24     arrays of the same size.
25
26     H = TTEST(...,ALPHA) performs the test at the significance level
27     (100*ALPHA)%. ALPHA must be a scalar.
28
29     H = TTEST(...,TAIL) performs the test against the alternative
30     hypothesis specified by TAIL:
31        'both'  -- "mean is not zero (or M)" (two-tailed test)
32        'right' -- "mean is greater than zero (or M)"
33                        (right-tailed test)
34        'left'  -- "mean is less than zero (or M)" (left-tailed test)
35     TAIL must be a single string.
36
```

(Continued)

(Continued)

```
37     [H,P] = TTEST(...) returns the p-value, i.e., the probability of
38     observing the given result, or one more extreme, by chance if the
39     null hypothesis is true. Small values of P cast doubt on the
40     validity of the null hypothesis.
41
42     [H,P,CI] = TTEST(...) returns a 100*(1-ALPHA)% confidence interval
43     for the true mean of X, or of X-Y for a paired test.
44
45     [H,P,CI,STATS] = TTEST(...) returns a structure with the
46     following fields:
47         'tstat' -- the value of the test statistic
48         'df'    -- the degrees of freedom of the test
49         'sd'    -- the estimated population standard deviation. For a
50                    paired test, this is the std. dev. of X-Y.
51
52         ...
```

7.2.1 One-Sample *t* test

Let's try using `ttest` to conduct a one-sample *t* test.

```
 1 >> [h,p,ci,stats]=ttest(ERs(:,1),.10)
 2 h =
 3     1
 4 p =
 5     0.0324
 6 ci =
 7     0.1048
 8     0.1974
 9 stats =
10     tstat: 2.3079
11        df: 19
12        sd: 0.0990
13 >> [h,p,ci,stats]=ttest(ERs(:,1),.15)
14 h =
15     0
16 p =
17     0.9620
18 ci =
19     0.1048
20     0.1974
21 stats =
22     tstat: 0.0482
23        df: 19
24        sd: 0.0990
```

It looks like the error rate for this condition is significantly different than .10 $[t(19) = 2.31, p < .05]$, but it is not statistically different than .15 $[t(19) = 0.05]$.

Now, some of you may not have access to the Statistics Toolbox, which is required to use `ttest`. While this will prove essential for you to conduct your research analyses in MATLAB, I wanted to give you a temporary solution so that you can still try and follow along with the examples in this book. To this end, I made a simplified version of `ttest` that was included with the functions that came with this book, called `imbttest`. If the `imbwelcome` command from Chapter 2 worked successfully, then you should be able to use `imbttest` fine. I have made `imbttest` such that its output follows the same structure as `ttest`.

```
 1 >> [h,p,ci,stats]=imbttest(ERs(:,1),.10)
 2 h =
 3      1
 4  p =
 5      0.0324
 6 ci =
 7      0.1048      0.1974
 8 stats =
 9      tstat: 2.3079
10         df: 19
11         sd: 0.0990
12 >> [h,p,ci,stats]=imbttest(ERs(:,1),.15)
13 h =
14      0
15 p =
16      0.9620
17 ci =
18      0.1048      0.1974
19 stats =
20      tstat: 0.0482
21         df: 19
22         sd: 0.0990
```

Note that the `imbttest` function can calculate *t* tests just as accurately as the `ttest` function but is unable to deal with NaNs and will give you less helpful error responses if you make a mistake.

```
 1 >> [h,p,ci,stats]=ttest(.10,ERs(:,1))
 2 ??? Error using ==> ttest at 68
 3 The data in a paired t-test must be the same size.
```

(Continued)

(Continued)

```
 4 >> [h,p,ci,stats]=imbttest(.10,ERs(:,1))
 5 h =
 6       1
 7 p =
 8       0
 9 ci =
10    -0.0511    -0.0511
11 stats =
12    tstat: -0.5161
13       df: 0
14       sd: 0.0990
```

Clearly, something has gone wrong when the degrees of freedom is zero.

7.2.2 Paired-Sample *t* test

Conducting a paired-sample *t* test is fairly straightforward; we simply provide two variables. Let's test if the error rates are different between the first and second conditions, and between the first and third conditions.

```
 1 >> [h,p,ci,stats]=ttest(ERs(:,1),ERs(:,2))
 2 h =
 3       0
 4 p =
 5       0.1411
 6 ci =
 7      -0.0066
 8       0.0430
 9 stats =
10    tstat: 1.5358
11       df: 19
12       sd: 0.0530
13 >> [h,p,ci,stats]=ttest(ERs(:,1),ERs(:,3))
14 h =
15       1
16 p =
17       0.0024
18 ci =
19       0.0193
20       0.0770
21 stats =
22    tstat: 3.4937
23       df: 19
24       sd: 0.0617
```

It looks like the difference is not statistically significant for the first comparison [$t(19) = 1.53$] but is significant for the second test [$t(19) = 3.49$, $p < .01$]. Note that if you were actually analyzing this data set for publication, you should correct for multiple comparisons.

`imbttest` also works for paired-sample t tests.

```
 1 >> [h,p,ci,stats]=imbttest(ERs(:,1),ERs(:,2))
 2 h =
 3       0
 4 p =
 5      0.1411
 6 ci =
 7      -0.0066     0.0430
 8 stats =
 9       tstat: 1.5358
10          df: 19
11          sd: 0.0530
12 >> [h,p,ci,stats]=imbttest(ERs(:,1),ERs(:,3))
13 h =
14       1
15 p =
16      0.0024
17 ci =
18      0.0193     0.0770
19 stats =
20       tstat: 3.4937
21          df: 19
22          sd: 0.0617
```

Again, `imbttest` is not built as well as `ttest,` as it is not able to best respond to improper inputs, such as when the two variables for the paired-sample comparison are not of the same length.

```
 1 >> [h,p,ci,stats]=ttest(ERs(:,1),ERs(1:10,3))
 2 ??? Error using ==> ttest at 68
 3 The data in a paired t-test must be the same size.
 4
 5 >> [h,p,ci,stats]=imbttest(ERs(:,1),ERs(1:10,3))
 6 ??? Error using ==> minus
 7 Matrix dimensions must agree.
 8
 9 Error in ==> imbttest at 17
10 sd = std(x - y);
```

7.2.3 Adjusting *t* test Parameters

Before we move on, I should also note that MATLAB also allows you to adjust your alpha level (default is .05) and which tail of the distribution you are testing (default is "both").

```
 1 >> [h,p,ci,stats]=ttest(ERs(:,1),ERs(:,3),.10)
 2 h =
 3      1
 4 p =
 5      0.0024
 6 ci =
 7      0.0243
 8      0.0720
 9 stats =
10      tstat: 3.4937
11         df: 19
12         sd: 0.0617
13 >> [h,p,ci,stats]=ttest(ERs(:,1),ERs(:,3),.05,'left')
14 h =
15      0
16 p =
17      0.9988
18 ci =
19        -Inf
20      0.0720
21 stats =
22      tstat: 3.4937
23         df: 19
24         sd: 0.0617
```

I have also built this functionality into `imbttest`.

```
 1 >> [h,p,ci,stats]=imbttest(ERs(:,1),ERs(:,3),.10)
 2 h =
 3      1
 4 p =
 5      0.0024
 6 ci =
 7      0.0243    0.0720
 8 stats =
 9      tstat: 3.4937
10         df: 19
11         sd: 0.0617
12 >> [h,p,ci,stats]=imbttest(ERs(:,1),ERs(:,3),.05,'left')
```

```
13 h =
14      0
15 p =
16      0.9988
17 ci =
18          -Inf    0.0720
19 stats =
20      tstat: 3.4937
21         df: 19
22         sd: 0.0617
```

7.3 Independent-Samples *t* test

`ttest` works great when we want to compare our data against a single value or do a repeated-measures test, but what if we want to compare two groups of participants? That's when `ttest2` comes in. The `ttest2` function allows us to make comparisons between independent samples. Let's load some of the data from the `worddb` data to try this out. Let's use `mkfigAro3.m` to load in the data.

```
1 >> mkfigAro3
```

If you take a look at the code, you might remember that the **types** variable has a list of our seven word types. To get the arousal ratings for all of the words of a given type, as noted in `mkfigAro3`, we can type the following:

```
1 worddata{18}(find(strcmp(worddata{2},types{i})))
```

where i is 1 to 7 corresponding to the seven word types.

Let's test if the arousal ratings for the negative low-arousal words significantly differ from the negative high-arousal words. One would think they should, given their labels, but let's do the stats on it.

```
1 >> [h,p,ci,stat]=ttest2(worddata{18}(find(strcmp(worddata{2},types{2}))), ...
2 worddata{18}(find(strcmp(worddata{2},types{1}))))
3 h =
4      1
5 p =
```

(Continued)

(Continued)

```
 6     2.6778e-07
 7 ci =
 8     -0.8511
 9     -0.4033
10 stat =
11       tstat: -5.5647
12          df: 90
13          sd: 0.5405
```

As we thought, this difference effect was quite statistically significant [$t(90) = 5.56, p < .001$].

As before, I have also made my own simplified version of ttest2, called imbttest2, which works equivalently.

```
 1 >> [h,p,ci,stat]=imbttest2(worddata{18}(find(strcmp(worddata{2}, ...
 2 types{2}))),worddata{18}(find(strcmp(worddata{2},types{1}))))
 3 h =
 4      1
 5 p =
 6     2.6778e-07
 7 ci =
 8     -0.8511    -0.4033
 9 stat =
10       tstat: -5.5647
11          df: 90
12          sd: 0.5405
```

Let's try another comparison: arousal ratings for negative high-arousal words versus positive high-arousal words.

```
 1 >> [h,p,ci,stat]=imbttest2(worddata{18}(find(strcmp(worddata{2}, ...
 2 types{1}))),worddata{18}(find(strcmp(worddata{2},types{3}))))
 3 h =
 4      0
 5 p =
 6     0.8566
 7 ci =
 8     -0.2556    0.3069
 9 stat =
10       tstat: 0.1812
11          df: 90
12          sd: 0.6790
```

Here the arousal ratings are not statistically different [$t(90) = 0.18$], which is good as they theoretically shouldn't be different.

As with `ttest`, `ttest2` can also have the alpha and tails manually set. `ttest2` also has the option to not assume that the two samples have equal variances (which is the default). Note that I did not include this functionality in `imbttest2`.

7.4 Correlation Does Not Imply Causation

Other than compare means (such as with a *t* test), your other main statistics tool as a behavioral researcher is correlations. Of course, MATLAB can also calculate correlations for us.

Let's calculate the correlation between our arousal ratings, for all words, with the ratings for tabooness (column 14) using the `corr` function.

```
1 >> [r,p]=corr(worddata{18}(1:460),worddata{14}(1:460))
2 r =
3     0.8352
4 p =
5   5.3639e-121
```

As you can see, the correlation between these two measures is statistically significant [$r(458) = .84, p < .001$]. Note that we had to specify the row numbers (1:460) to ignore the NaNs from the nonword rows at the end of the data file. Unless specified otherwise, `corr` calculates the Pearson product-moment correlation

One other MATLAB function can also be used to calculate the Pearson product-moment correlation, `corrcoef`.

```
1 >> [r,p]=corrcoef(worddata{18}(1:460),worddata{14}(1:460))
2 r =
3     1.0000    0.8352
4     0.8352    1.0000
5 p =
6     1.0000    0.0000
7     0.0000    1.0000
```

`corrcoef` is made for calculating correlations between matrices of data, so I personally tend to use `corr`.

Again, I have also included a correlation function that does not require the Statistics Toolbox with this book, `imbcorr`. As usual, this function works similarly to `corr` but is a bit less flexible.

```
1 >> [r,p]=imbcorr(worddata{18}(1:460),worddata{14}(1:460))
2 r =
3     0.8352
4 p =
5     0
```

Let's also try and calculate the correlation between arousal and valence (column 16) ratings.

```
1 >> [r,p]=corr(worddata{18}(1:460),worddata{16}(1:460))
2 r =
3    -0.3766
4 p =
5    6.0231e-17
```

Even though this correlation is statistically significant, note that the relationship between arousal and valence is largely nonlinear, as illustrated in Figure 4.7 (p. 78). This correlation likely was significant partly due to the sheer number of data points we have. With enough data points, almost any effect can be significant. Keep this in mind as you do your own analyses!

> **★ TIP #37**
>
> If you use correlations quite a bit, you may also want to look into `partialcorr`. ∎

7.5 Nonparametric Correlations

If you want to calculate correlations for data sets that may not be normally distributed or have other reasons to calculate nonparametric correlations, you usually want to conduct a Spearman's rank-order correlation (ρ). This can be done in MATLAB by specifying the type of correlation in `corr` as Spearman. Let's try this with the arousal–tabooness correlation.

```
1 >> [rho,p]=corr(worddata{18}(1:460),worddata{14}(1:460), ...
2 'type','Spearman')
3 rho =
4     0.7403
5 p =
6     5.1892e-81
```

If you are lacking the Statistics Toolbox, I also wrote `imbspear` so you won't feel too left out.

```
1 >> [rho,p]=imbspear(worddata{18}(1:460),worddata{14}(1:460))
2 rho =
3     0.7466
4 p =
5     0
```

Unlike the `imbttest`, `imbttest2`, and `imbcorr`, my version of this function involved approximations that make it less precise than MATLAB's version.

7.6 Additional Statistical Tests

The Statistics Toolbox also includes a number of other functions that may be of use to a behavioral researcher. Some of these are the tests for nonparametric comparisons of means and medians such as the `ranksum` function, which calculates the the Wilcoxon rank-sum test (and is equivalent to the Mann–Whitney U test), and the `signrank` function, which is the Wilcoxon signed-rank test. There are also several functions for testing of normality: `kstest`, `kstest2`, and `jbtest`.

7.7 Bootstrapping

When your data are *not* normally distributed, it isn't appropriate to calculate your confidence intervals based on standard deviations. As this is not a statistics textbook, I won't get into *why* this is so but will instead show you how to use bootstrapping to determine confidence intervals for a median and for statistics such as correlations.

First, let's calculate the `mean` and `median` arousal ratings for the taboo words.

```
 1 >> types
 2 types =
 3      'neg hi ar'
 4      'neg lo ar'
 5      'pos hi ar'
 6      'pos lo ar'
 7      'rel neu'
 8      'taboo'
 9      'unrel neu'
10 >> mean(worddata{18}(find(strcmp(worddata{2},types{6}))))
11 ans =
12      4.3357
13 >> median(worddata{18}(find(strcmp(worddata{2},types{6}))))
14 ans =
15      4.3400
```

It looks like the `mean` and `median` ratings here are almost identical. In that case, we might also expect their confidence intervals to also be similar.

For the 95% confidence interval of the mean, we can use a code similar to what we determined earlier:

```
1 >> mAroTab = mean(worddata{18}(find(strcmp(worddata{2},types{6}))));
2 >> stdAroTab = std(worddata{18}(find(strcmp(worddata{2},types{6}))));
3 >> nAroTab = length(find(strcmp(worddata{2},types{6})));
4 >> ciAroTab= stdAroTab/sqrt(nAroTab)*1.96;
5 >> [ mAroTab-ciAroTab mAroTab+ciAroTab ]
6 ans =
7     4.1334  4.5379
```

Now, here are the principles of bootstrapping: Bootstrapping involves taking a sample of data points from your data set, where the number of samples is the same as the number of data points you have, but you sample *with replacement*. Since you are sampling with replacement, you will have multiples of some data points, and others will be missing from this sample. You then take your statistic of this sample, such as calculating the median. This procedure is repeated many times, usually around 10,000 times.

First, we'll set our number of iterations (i.e., repetitions of this sampling procedure).

```
1 >> iter = 10000;
```

As a test, let's try sampling with replacement. The easiest way is to use rand to generate numbers that correspond to our data points.

```
 1 >> rand(nAroTab,1)
 2 ans =
 3      0.3112
 4      0.5285
 5      0.1656
 6      0.6020
 7      0.2630
 8      ...
 9 >> ceil(rand(nAroTab,1)*nAroTab)
10 ans =
11      57
12      80
13      75
14      54
15      17
16      ...
```

Next, we need to find the median for these words.

```
1 >> AroTab = worddata{18}(find(strcmp(worddata{2},types{6})));
2 >> median(AroTab(sample))
3 ans =
4     4.1650
```

For the real code, we will use a for loop to repeat this for iter times.

```
1 for i = 1:iter
2     sample = ceil(rand(nAroTab,1)*nAroTab);
3     bootAroTab(i) = median(AroTab(sample));
4 end
```

Now, bootAroTab is quite long.

```
1 >> bootAroTab
2 ans =
3   Columns 1 through 6
4     4.5350    4.6200    4.3850    4.1900    4.2900    4.2900
5   Columns 7 through 12
6     4.2950    4.3900    4.4300    4.1400    4.1900    4.2350
7     ...
```

```
1 >> length(bootAroTab)
2 ans =
3        10000
```

If we sort the contents of **bootAroTab** and then look at entries 250 and 9750, these would correspond to the 2.5 and 97.5 percentile bounds.

```
1 >> bootAroTab = sort(bootAroTab);
2 >> bootAroTab([250 9750])
3 ans =
4     4.0150    4.6200
```

And now we would have the 95% confidence intervals for the median!

To make the code a bit more general, such as if **iter** is not set to 1,000, we can use the percentiles directly.

```
1 >> [round(.025*iter) round(.975*iter)]
2 ans =
3           250         9750
4 >> bootAroTab([round(.025*iter) round(.975*iter)])
5 ans =
6     4.0150    4.6200
```

All of the essential code, without the explorations along the way, can be put together as below.

```
1 AroTab = worddata{18}(find(strcmp(worddata{2},types{6})));
2
3 iter = 10000;
4
5 for i = 1:iter
6     sample = ceil(rand(nAroTab,1)*nAroTab);
7     bootAroTab(i) = median(AroTab(sample));
8 end
9
10 bootAroTab = sort(bootAroTab);
11
12 bootAroTab([round(.025*iter) round(.975*iter)])
```

Bootstrapping can be an extremely useful statistical tool. Hopefully, you've learned a bit more about it in this section!

7.8 Restructuring Data

Sometimes our data are not in quite the right arrangement for our analyses. For instance, say we want to calculate the standard deviation of a set of numbers that is arranged as a matrix. Unfortunately, it's a bit hard to come up with a relatable example for this, so here we'll just use `rand`.

```
1 >> M=rand(5,4)
2 M =
3      0.7577      0.7060      0.8235      0.4387
4      0.7431      0.0318      0.6948      0.3816
5      0.3922      0.2769      0.3171      0.7655
6      0.6555      0.0462      0.9502      0.7952
7      0.1712      0.0971      0.0344      0.1869
```

If we simply use the `std` function, we can only get the standard deviation along one dimension or the other.

```
 1 >> std(M)
 2 ans =
 3      0.2548      0.2826      0.3791      0.2610
 4 >> std(M,[],2)
 5 ans =
 6      0.1688
 7      0.3290
 8      0.2236
 9      0.3958
10      0.0705
```

To get the standard deviation, or any other measure, across the full matrix, we will need to use the **reshape** function. Simply, `reshape` will 'reshape' the values in your variable such that their organization across rows, columns, and other dimensions matches your new specifications. As you might expect, the total number of values ('area') in your matrix must remain constant. Let's explore this a bit.

```
 1 >> M1=reshape(M,2,10)
 2 M1 =
 3   Columns 1 through 6
 4      0.7577     0.3922     0.1712     0.0318     0.0462     0.8235
 5      0.7431     0.6555     0.7060     0.2769     0.0971     0.6948
 6   Columns 7 through 10
 7      0.3171     0.0344     0.3816     0.7952
 8      0.9502     0.4387     0.7655     0.1869
 9 >> M2=reshape(M,20,1)
10 M2 =
11      0.7577
12      0.7431
13      0.3922
14      0.6555
15      0.1712
16      0.7060
17      0.0318
18      0.2769
19      0.0462
20      0.0971
21      0.8235
22      0.6948
23      0.3171
24      0.9502
25      0.0344
26      0.4387
27      0.3816
28      0.7655
29      0.7952
30      0.1869
```

If we test the `size`, we can see that it always remains consistent.

```
1 >> size(M)
2 ans =
3      5     4
4 >> size(M1)
5 ans =
6      2    10
7 >> size(M2)
8 ans =
9     20     1
```

Using the prod function, we can easily check that the area of the matrix is constant. prod simply multiplies a series of values together, similar to how sum adds values.

```
1 >> prod(size(M))
2 ans =
3    20
4 >> prod(size(M1))
5 ans =
6    20
7 >> prod(size(M2))
8 ans =
9    20
```

Now, to answer the original question, we can calculate the standard deviation across all 20 values.

```
1 >> std(M2)
2 ans =
3     0.3070
```

This can also be done all in one step:

```
1 >> std(reshape(M,20,1))
2 ans =
3     0.3070
```

Along somewhat similar lines there is one other fairly useful function: squeeze. Briefly, squeeze reshapes the contents of a variable such that if any matrix has a dimension that is only one in length, that dimension will be removed. Let's give this a try.

```
1 >> M3=rand(5,1,4)
2 M3(:,:,1) =
3      0.4898
4      0.4456
5      0.6463
6      0.7094
7      0.7547
8 M3(:,:,2) =
9      0.2760
10     0.6797
11     0.6551
12     0.1626
13     0.1190
```

(Continued)

(Continued)

```
14 M3(:,:,3) =
15      0.4984
16      0.9597
17      0.3404
18      0.5853
19      0.2238
20 M3(:,:,4) =
21      0.7513
22      0.2551
23      0.5060
24      0.6991
25      0.8909
26 >> squeeze(M3)
27 ans =
28      0.4898    0.2760    0.4984    0.7513
29      0.4456    0.6797    0.9597    0.2551
30      0.6463    0.6551    0.3404    0.5060
31      0.7094    0.1626    0.5853    0.6991
32      0.7547    0.1190    0.2238    0.8909
```

This function may seem fairly abstract now, but it is a good one to know about before you need it. Additionally, it is unlikely you would ever otherwise come across `squeeze`, by other means, such as `lookfor`.

7.9 Further Analyses

The analyses that you use for your research are likely to extend beyond t tests and correlations. MATLAB is capable of many other statistical analyses using the Statistics Toolbox (such as ANOVAs: `anova1`, `anova2`), and you can also look for functions written by others (see Section 9.2.2). That being said, while it is preferable to do all your analyses in MATLAB, it can sometimes be easier to continue your analyses in another program such as IBM SPSS, R, or SigmaPlot. If you have forgotten how to export your data from MATLAB, see Section 2.9.

EXERCISES

Time for the exercises to see how much you've learned! Now that we have learned statistics, your introduction to MATLA is almost complete.

1. Using all participants in the decision1 data set, do a *t* test to see if error rates were significantly different between the 1 s and 2 s delay conditions.

2. Conduct a *t* test to see if the motion direction affects error rates, regardless of delay condition (i.e., on the same values as calculated in Chapter 5, Question 3).

3. Load the `worddb` data. Is there any difference in the offensiveness of high-arousal negative and positive words?

4. How strong is the correlation between word familiarity and personal use, across all word types?

5. What is the correlation between arousal and valence? Test if it is valid to use a Pearson correlation or if a nonparametric correlation would be more appropriate.

6. Adjust the `freq` function you wrote in Chapter 5, Question 4 such that it will also work for strings as well as numbers. Use this modified function to count the number of words of each word type in the `worddb` data set. Also test that it still works for the decision1 data as well (testing only the first participant is sufficient).

See page 210 for the solutions. Next up: Practice using all of our training to work through a handful of new data sets.

FUNCTION REVIEW

General: `reshape prod squeeze`

Statistics: `ttest ttest2 corr corrcoef`

8

Putting It All Together

You now have a good understanding of MATLAB and have begun to see its applications to behavioral research. Now, it's time to test your knowledge. In this chapter, I will give you new data sets and new problems, all of which you should be able to solve. You may need to use `help` at times, and the exercises with these next data sets will test your MATLAB abilities to the limit. Now, it is time we work on generalizing your MATLAB skills from the few data sets you've been using thus far to more real-world problems. Final answers—not steps—are included at the end of the book, as with previous exercises. If you're still not confident in your MATLAB abilities, you may want to work through earlier examples again and come back later.

List of the Exercises

8.1 Another Look at Decision-Making Data

Let's start with something easy. The `decision1` data set that was introduced in Chapter 5 was the first experiment of Bogacz et al. (2010). The paper also included a second experiment, and the data are in a very similar format. Let's see if you can work through the main analyses here without referring back to the earlier chapters too much.

In this experiment, participants were presented a 10 × 10 grid on a computer monitor. Cells of this grid were randomly filled with asterisks, and the participant had to judge if the majority of the cells were filled or empty. Trials where 40 or 60 cells were filled were coded as "easy", while trials where 47 or 53 cells were filled were coded as "difficult".

The data for 20 participants from this study can be found in the `decision2` folder. Variable names used in the `.mat` files are identical to those used in `decision1`, with the addition of the variable `Anum` (asterisk number). The complete list of variable descriptions is given below and in `data_legend.txt`.

```
 1 blocknum - number of block within the experiment, during which the
 2       trial was performed
 3 trialnum - number of trial within the block
 4 D - the delay between the response on this trial and onset of the
 5     next trial
 6 Dpen - additional penalty delay for making an error
 7 ST - binary vector describing the stimulus on the given trial,
 8     i.e. whether dots were moving leftwards or rightwards
 9 ER - binary vector describing whether participant made
10     incorrect response on this trial
11 RT - reaction time on the given trial [in seconds]
12
13 Anum - diffuculty of a trial: 60=easy, 53=difficult
```

1. What is the mean error rate for the first participant, for the easy and difficult trials, regardless of delay?

2. Calculate the mean error rates and reaction times for the easy trials, for each of the four delay conditions, for only the first participant. The delay times are the same as in `decision1`. Repeat for the difficult trials.

3. Find the mean error rates and reaction times, for all of the eight conditions, for each of the 20 participants provided.

4. Adjust the code from Question 3 to only use RTs from trials that were correct.

5. Based on the output from Question 4, determine the mean and SEM for each condition's error rate, across the sample of 20 participants.

6. Make a bar plot with error bars for the error rates.

7. Adjust the bar plot to increase the readability: bigger text and thicker lines. Also adjust the *y*-axis tick marks to have the same number of decimal places.

8.2 A Simple Mathematical Simulation

Hopefully, that exercise wasn't too bad. For this next example, we'll start to push our boundaries a bit and do a simple simulation exercise.

1. In this exercise, we want a simple coin-tossing simulation, given two constraints: (a) coin tosses must result in either heads (1) or tails (0) as the only possible outcomes, and (b) the number of tosses in the simulation can be set in a variable.

2. Try and implement Exercise 1 *without* using a `for` (or `while`) loop.

3. Write a code to easily check how many times the outcome was heads or tails.

4. Write a function to calculate the running mean across *n* number of or trials.

5. Take the code from Questions 3 and 4 and adjust it to work for a six-sided die instead. ("Die" is singular for dice!) Possible outcomes now should be 1 to 6.

6. Can you make your code more flexible such that it can work for an *n*-sided die? (In other words, make the number of sides of the die a variable that can be adjusted.)

7. Can you make your code from Question 6 simpler by using `max`? (*Hint*: You may need to use `help`.)

Hopefully, you again see that there are multiple ways to implement a given problem within MATLAB.

8.3 Correlations and Scatterplots

Our next data set is another word database, the Bristol norms for age of acquisition (AoA), imageability, and familiarity (Stadthagen-Gonzalez & Davis, 2006). AoA is a rating of the age at which a word would have been learned. (Imageability and familiarity were previously defined when the `worddb` database was introduced.) This database consists of ratings for these three-word properties for a total of 1,526 words and will be referred to here as the `bristol` data set. Feel free to refer to the original paper for further details about the data set.

For your convenience, below is a list of the columns in this data file.

```
 1  WORD
 2  AoA (Yrs)
 3  AoA (100-700)
 4  IMG
 5  FAM
 6  LEN_L
 7  LEN_S
 8  LEN_P
 9  MLBF
10  N
```

1. Open the data text file (in the `bristol` data folder) and see how it is formatted. Load this data set into MATLAB.

2. Make a scatterplot of the imageability and familiarity ratings.

3. Calculate the correlation between the age of acquisition and imageability. Here, we will use the AoA rating that is in years (rather than the 100–700 range).

4. Is there any correlation between age of acquisition and word length? Compute this correlation for all three measures of word length included in this database. (As reported in the paper: LEN_L = word length in letters; LEN_S = word length in syllables; LEN_P = word length in phonemes.)

5. Which words have the highest and lowest AoAs? Which are the respective AoA values?

6. What are the top 10 most and least imageable words in this database?

7. Compare the imageability ratings for the 100 highest and lowest AoA words using a t test.

8.4 Visualizing Two-Dimensional Responses: Part I

Our next data set will push your MATLAB skills further. In Gray and Spetch (2006), pigeons were trained to search for a hidden goal location in a two-dimensional spatial arrangement based on one of two strategies: (1) to use landmarks within the spatial arrangement ("Landmark" group) or (2) to use walls as the cues for the goal location ("Wall" group). As a test to see how these two strategies affected pigeons' search behavior, the arrangement was expanded, referred to as "expansion tests." Though search behavior did not differ between groups on this test, here we will try and reproduce the "Expansion" panels of Figure 1 of the Gray and Spetch (2006) paper. We will start with some partially analyzed data: the raw number of searches in 10 cm × 10 cm grid sections for each bird. In the case of the expansion tests, the grid area consisted of 10 × 10 grid sections. The data from the expansion tests can be found in the 2dpeck data folder with the "Grid Section" following the numbering shown below on the left.

91	92	93	94	95	96	97	98	99	100
81	82	83	84	85	86	87	88	89	90
71	72	73	74	75	76	77	78	79	80
61	62	63	64	65	66	67	68	69	70
51	52	53	54	55	56	57	58	59	60
41	42	43	44	45	46	47	48	49	50
31	32	33	34	35	36	37	38	39	40
21	22	23	24	25	26	27	28	29	30
11	12	13	14	15	16	17	18	19	20
1	2	3	4	5	6	7	8	9	10

1. Load the data.

2. Calculate the proportion of searches in each grid section for each bird, for the Landmark group. Average these proportions across birds. Check that the proportions sum to 1.

3. Create a figure of the search pattern similar to Figure 1 of the Gray and Spetch (2006) paper. My own version of this figure is shown above and on the right.

4. When saving the figure created from your code above, you may have had trouble making sure the figure was exactly square. Though you may have manually tried to adjust it, your attempt was likely still imprecise. Use the function `fillpage` included with this book to adjust the page size of the figure and make the figure perfectly square, as it should be. Learn to use `fillpage` using `help`. (*Note*: `fillpage` was obtained from the MATLAB File Exchange; see Section 9.2.2 for more details.)

5. Make a script that can easily create figures for both groups.

6. Reproduce the labelled grid image above. (*Hint*: You should use the `text` function.)

8.5 Visualizing Two-Dimensional Responses: Part II

One other relatively common type of two-dimensional spatial data is images and eye-tracking responses. In this example data set, we will use some of the data from the Fixations In FAce (FIFA; `http://www.klab.caltech.edu/~moran/fifadb/`) database (Cerf, Harel, Einhaeuser, & Koch, 2007). For this example, we will need to extend our expertise to include some of the functions in the Image Processing Toolbox. The data from this example can be found in the `eyetrack` data folder.

1. Load image 0001.jpg. (*Hint*: Look into the `imread` and `imshow` functions.)

2. Shown below is a description of the data files as described on the FIFA website. (This is also saved as `data_legend.txt` in the `eyetrack` data folder.)

```
 1 The fixations struct contains the following data for each image:
 2 sbj{i} - subject number (1-9)
 3 ... .age - subject age at the time they participated in the
 4            experiment
 5 ... .sex - m - male; f - female
 6 ... .response - an array (1-200) of numbers corresponding to the
 7                 subject rating of the image (1-9); ordered by
 8                 imgList
 9 ... .order - the order by which the images were seen by the
10              subject in the actual experiment.
11 Example: find(sbj{1}.order == 16) returns 159, indicating that
12          the 159th image the subject saw was imgList{16}.
13 ... .scan{j} - scanpath for each image (1-200). The
14               corresponding images names are listed in imgList{j}
15 ... ... .fix_x - the x location of the fixations (number of
16                  fixations vary per image. fix_x(2) refers to
```

```
17                     the second fixation.
18 ... ... .fix_y - the y location of the fixations
19 ... ... .fix_duration - the duration (in milliseconds) of each
20                         fixation.
21 ... ... .scan_x - the x location of the saccade. We acquired for
22                 2 seconds at 1000Hz.
23 ... ... .scan_y - the y location of the saccade.
24
25 The imgList struct contains the following data for each image:
26 imgList{i} - the name of the image (1-200).
27
28 The annotations struct contains the following data for
29 each image:
30 an{i} - the annotation of the image, corresponding to imgList{i}.
31 ... .objects{j} - the object annotations (number of objects in
32                  each image vary)
33 ... ... .name - the labeling of the object ('Face','Phone',
34                  'Banana', etc.)
35 ... ... .mask - the location of the annotated object.
```

Using the `annotations.mat` file, adjust the image such that the face is highlighted.

3. Make a function that can plot the fixations of all subjects on top of the original image. Make the size of the fixation marker in your figure proportional to the fixation duration. Compare your output image from your function with the resulting image below for image 1.

Source: Cerf et al. (2007).

Additional answer images for images 10 and 16 are included in the solutions section (pp. 234–235).

4. Can you come up with a way to visualize the raw eye positions, such as using a heat map? For now, let's just plot it as a different panel of the same figure. (Start from the code you made in response to Question 3.)

5. Using the code from Question 4, can you instead find a way to plot the eye positions on top of the actual image?

6. In vision research, it can also often be useful to present participants with scrambled images, as these images contain the same color and luminance properties as the original image, but no longer contain form information (e.g., faces, objects). Though scrambled images weren't used in the FIFA study, let's try scrambling some of these images ourselves. Along with this book I've included a function called `randblock`, which was also obtained from the MATLAB File Exchange (see Section 9.2.2). Learn how to use `randblock` and create versions of `0001.jpg` that have blocks of size (a) 256 pixels, (b) 64 pixels, (c) 16 pixels, and (d) 1 pixels. Save these scrambled images using `imwrite`.

8.6 Counterbalancing Conditions for an Experiment

For our last exercise, we will try and create a pseudorandomized sequence of trials. Here, we will try and make a list of trials that follow a list of predefined rules but are otherwise random and save this list as a text file. This file can then be later imported into a stimulus presentation program such as E-Prime (`http://www.pstnet.com`) and Presentation (`http://www.neurobs.com`). This can be particularly useful as sometimes important pseudorandomization constraints may not be easily implementable in these software packages directly, whereas here we would pre-generate the trial sequences in MATLAB for later use.

1. Generate a pseudorandomized list of 48 trials consisting of four experimental conditions, given the constraint that no condition can occur three times in a row.

2. Implement a second-level factor (i.e., ITI) that is nested within the earlier four experiment conditions.

3. Save the trial information to a text file and make a figure to illustrate the trial sequence.

4. Recode the `seq` and `iti` variables into a single value for each trial (i.e., a number from 1–8). Also write a script to convert this value back into the separate `seq` and `iti` variables. (*Hint*: `mod` may be useful here.)

9

THE FINAL CHAPTER

9.1 The Beginning of the End

Congratulations; you've made it to the end of the book!

When you began this journey, most of you knew nothing about MATLAB. Now, you don't know everything, but you should definitely know enough to get you started in implementing any analyses you may want to try. If you get stuck, don't be afraid to try sifting through some of MATLAB's documentation (especially `doc` and `lookfor`) or searching on the Internet. Rarely are you the first person to encounter a particular analysis issue, especially if you can think of it in more general terms.

> **★ TIP #38**
>
> If you're not sure why you're doing a particular analysis in MATLAB anymore, you may want to consult the MATLAB function `why`. It may not provide you with the answer you were looking for, but it is a fun little Easter egg built into MATLAB. ∎

9.2 Further Directions

9.2.1 Official Toolboxes

Now that you're reasonably adept with MATLAB, there are a number of additional toolboxes that have been created by The MathWorks that may be helpful to your research and that your university may even already have a license for. The most essential toolbox for a behavioral researcher is the Statistics Toolbox, covered in Chapter 7. Along with it, several others worth noting include the following:

- Curve Fitting Toolbox: It is useful for fitting a "curve," that is, a mathematical function (polynomial, exponential, etc.) to a data set. It includes a relatively helpful GUI. If you have it (e.g., from a university site license), the most helpful starting point would be to try the `cftool` function.
- Optimization Toolbox: It is useful for more complicated model fitting, particularly nonlinear models that cannot be applied through the curve fitting toolbox. In my own practice, I mainly use `fminsearch`.
- Neural Network Toolbox: I haven't used this toolbox personally, but I'm sure it is of benefit to some behavioral researchers. If you're not sure what a neural network is, feel free to leave this toolbox alone for now.
- Image Processing Toolbox: It is necessary when working with images (e.g., `imread`, `imshow`). It is particularly useful for vision researchers (e.g., to convert from RGB to LAB color spaces, start with `makecform`).
- Parallel Computing Toolbox: It is used for complex mathematical simulations. Start with `matlabpool` and `parfor`.

In addition to the above toolboxes, several other MATLAB toolboxes developed by The MathWorks may be of use to behavioral researchers, such as the Econometrics Toolbox, the Wavelet Toolbox, and the Symbolic Math Toolbox.

9.2.2 MATLAB File Exchange

The MathWorks Inc. has made a wide variety of toolboxes for MATLAB, but we can't expect them to make everything we might need. To this end, The MathWorks Inc. maintains an online file exchange, the MATLAB File Exchange, where MATLAB users can post MATLAB scripts, functions, and toolboxes that they think may be useful to others. Take a look and see if anything catches your eye:

http://www.mathworks.com/matlabcentral/fileexchange/

Two functions used toward the end of this book, `fillpage` (p. 182) and `randblock` (p. 184), were obtained from the MATLAB File Exchange.

9.2.3 Extending MATLAB Through Third-Party Toolboxes

As hinted at in the previous section, other users have made a number of toolboxes for MATLAB (i.e., third-party toolboxes). Some of these are of particular use to behavioral researchers:

Stimulus presentation: In addition to analyzing your behavioral data, MATLAB can also be used to run your actual experiment! The main two toolboxes for implementing behavioral experiments are the Psychtoolbox (also referred to as the Psychophysics Toolbox; `http://psychtoolbox.org`) and Cogent 2000 (`http://www.vislab.ucl.ac.uk/cogent_2000.php`). Other similar toolboxes also exist, including the BioPsychology Toolbox (`http://biopsytoolbox.sourceforge.net`) and MGL (`http://gru.brain.riken.jp/doku.php?id=mgl:overview`).

Model-based behavioral analysis: There are also a few toolboxes designed to help fit formal, computational models to behavioral data, such as the Diffusion Model Analysis Toolbox (`http://ppw.kuleuven.be/okp/software/dmat/`), which is designed to model response time and error rate data from decision-making tasks. Other toolboxes include the Matlab Topic Modeling Toolbox (`http://psiexp.ss.uci.edu/research/programs_data/toolbox.htm`)—a model of semantic "topics," Palamedes (`http://www.palamedestoolbox.org`)—a toolbox for psychophysical data, and OXlearn (`http://psych.brookes.ac.uk/oxlearn/`)—a toolbox for neural network/connectionist modelling, as well as numerous others.

Neuroimaging data analysis: If your research instead leans more toward cognitive neuroscience, you're in luck! There are a number of third-party MATLAB toolboxes for neuroimaging data analyses. Most notably, fMRI, EEG, and MEG researchers can take advantage of SPM (`http://www.fil.ion.ucl.ac.uk/spm/`). EEG and MEG researchers can also use EEGLAB (`http://sccn.ucsd.edu/eeglab/`), FieldTrip (`http://fieldtrip.fcdonders.nl`), BrainStorm (`http://neuroimage.usc.edu/brainstorm/`), and the Mass Univariate ERP Toolbox (`http://openwetware.org/wiki/Mass_Univariate_ERP_Toolbox`).

There are also a number of toolboxes designed for analyzing eye-tracking data, including iMAP (`http://perso.unifr.ch/roberto.caldara/`) and GazeAlyze (`http://gazealyze.sourceforge.net/`).

> ★ **TIP #39**
>
> If you're considering using any third-party toolboxes, you may want to look into addpath, removepath, and path. startup may also be of particular use. ▪

9.3 Data Analysis Without MATLAB

Though you are now beginning to be quite fluent in MATLAB, there are a number of free alternatives that may be able to provide similar functionality, depending on your needs: Octave (http://www.gnu.org/software/octave/), Scilab (http://www.scilab.org), and FreeMat (http://freemat.sourceforge.net).

There are some differences in function names and syntax between MATLAB and these alternatives, but MATLAB is by no means better simply because it's expensive. However, seeing as you've managed to make it to the end of this book, you should be more than qualified to evaluate these software packages for yourself, if you so choose. Simply try an Internet search of comparisons between MATLAB and some of the programs listed above.

Several other programs that are notably less similar to MATLAB, but can serve similar purposes, include R (http://www.r-project.org), Scipy (http://www.scipy.org/), and Sage (http://www.sagemath.org).

9.3.1 Octave

Of your alternate options, Octave is definitely the most similar to MATLAB. To increase Octave's compatibility with MATLAB code, you can start Octave with the **traditional** option.

For further details also see http://en.wikibooks.org/wiki/MATLAB_Programming/Differences_between_Octave_and_MATLAB.

Note: The Psychtoolbox is designed to be compatible with Octave.

Appendix A

References

Bogacz, R., Hu, P. T., Holmes, P., & Cohen, J. D. (2010). Do humans produce the speed-accuracy tradeoff that maximizes reward rate? *Quarterly Journal of Experimental Psychology, 63*, 863–891.

Cerf, M., Harel, J., Einhaeuser, W., &. Koch, C. (2007). Predicting human gaze using low-level saliency combined with face detection. In *Advances in Neural Information Processing Systems (NIPS),* (vol. 20, pp. 241–248). Cambridge, MA: MIT Press.

Gray, E. R., & Spetch, M. L. (2006). Pigeons encode absolute distance but relational direction from landmarks and walls. *Journal of Experimental Psychology: Animal Behavior Processes, 32*, 474–480.

Janschewitz, K. (2008). Taboo, emotionally-valenced, and emotionally-neutral word norms. *Behavior Research Methods, 40*, 1065–1074.

Stadthagen-Gonzalez, H., & Davis, C. J. (2006). The Bristol norms for age of acquisition, imageability, and familiarity. *Behavior Research Methods, 38*, 598–605.

Willerman, L., Schultz, R., Rutledge, J. N., & Bigler, E. (1991). In vivo brain size and intelligence. *Intelligence, 15*, 223–228.

APPENDIX B

EXERCISE SOLUTIONS

Note that while these are the answers provided with the book, there are often many ways to arrive at the same solution.

Question 1

```
1 >> iqbrain(10,1)
2 ans =
3     133
```

Question 2

```
1 >> iqbrain(1:3,2)
2 ans =
3      816932
4     1001121
5     1038437
```

Question 3

```
1 >> iqbrain([5 9],:)
2 ans =
3        137      951545
4         89      904858
```

Question 4

```
1 >> (iqbrain(1,1) + iqbrain(2,1) + iqbrain(3,1)) / 3
2 ans =
3    137.3333
```

If you've already worked ahead, a "better" answer would be:

```
1 >> mean(iqbrain(1:3,1))
2 ans =
3    137.3333
```

Question 5

```
1 >> (iqbrain(8,2) + iqbrain(10,2)) / 2
2 ans =
3       904862
```

Again, a better answer would be:

```
1 >> mean(iqbrain([8 10],2))
2 ans =
3       904862
```

Question 6

```
1 >> iqbrain(7,2) / iqbrain(7,1)
2 ans =
3    7.1834e+03
```

Question 7

```
1 >> iqbrain(:,1) ./ iqbrain(:,2)
2 ans =
3    1.0e-03 *
4      0.1628
5      0.1398
6      0.1339
7      0.1378
8      0.1440
9      0.1066
10     0.1392
```

```
11      0.1077
12      0.0984
13      0.1392
```

Chapter 2

Question 1

```
1 >> cd('~/Desktop/matlabintro')
2 >> mkdir('ch2test')
```

Question 2

```
1 >> cd('ch2test')
2 >> dir
3 .    ..
4 >> cd('..')
```

Question 3

```
1 >> string = pwd
2 string =
3 /Users/chris/Desktop/matlabintro
```

Question 4

```
1 >> cd('~/Desktop/matlabintro')
2 >> cd('iqbrain')
3 >> load('data.txt')
```

Question 5

```
1 >> cd('~/Desktop/matlabintro')
2 >> cd('worddb')
3 >> fid = fopen('JanschewitzB386appB.txt','r');
4 >> formatstring = [ '%s %s' rempat(' %f',1,19) ];
5 >> worddata=textscan(fid,formatstring,'headerlines',5, ...
6 'delimiter','\t');
7 >> fclose(fid);
```

Chapter 3

Question 1

```
1 >> sum(data(:,1)==2)
2 ans =
3     20
```

Another valid answer:

```
1 >> length(find(data(:,1)==2))
2 ans =
3     20
```

Question 2

```
1 >> nanmean(data(:,4))
2 ans =
3     68.5256
4 >> nanmax(data(:,4))
5 ans =
6     77
7 >> nanmin(data(:,4))
8 ans =
9     62
```

If you don't have, or don't want to use, the NaN-friendly functions:

```
1 >> mean(data(find(~isnan(data(:,4))),4))
2 ans = 3
3     68.5256
4 >> max(data(find(~isnan(data(:,4))),4))
5 ans =
6     77
7 >> min(data(find(~isnan(data(:,4))),4))
8 ans =
9     62
```

Question 3

```
1 >> [height,id]=nanmax(data(:,4))
2 height=
3     77
```

```
4 id =
5      28
6 >> data(id,3)
7 ans =
8     187
```

If you don't have, or don't want to use, the NaN-friendly functions:

```
1 >> data(find(data(:,4)==max(data(find(~isnan(data(:,4))),4))),3)
2 ans =
3     187
```

Question 4

```
 1 >> fid = fopen('JanschewitzB386appB.txt','r');
 2 >> formatstring = [ '%s %s' repmat (' %f',1,19) ];
 3 >> worddata=textscan(fid,formatstring,'headerlines',5, ...
 4 'delimiter','\t');
 5 >> fclose(fid);
 6 >> [pos,id]=max(worddata{16})
 7 pos =
 8      8.0500
 9 id =
10     168
11 >> worddata{1}(id)
12 ans =
13     'loved'
```

Question 5

```
 1 >> [pers,id]=max(worddata{8})
 2 pers =
 3      8.0100
 4 id =
 5     158
 6 >> worddata{1}(id)
 7 ans =
 8     'food'
 9 >> [fam,id]=max(worddata{10})
10 fam =
11      8.1800
12 id =
13     158
14 >> worddata{1}(id)
15 ans =
16     'food'
```

Question 6

```
 1 >> types=unique(worddata{2}(1:460))
 2 types =
 3     'neg hi ar'
 4     'neg lo ar'
 5     'pos hi ar'
 6     'pos lo ar'
 7     'rel neu'
 8     'taboo'
 9     'unrel neu'
10 >> val(1) = mean(worddata{16}(find(strcmp(worddata{2},types(1)))))
11 val =
12     3.2009
13 >> val(2) = mean(worddata{16}(find(strcmp(worddata{2},types(2)))))
14 val =
15     3.2009    3.3896
16 >> val(3) = mean(worddata{16}(find(strcmp(worddata{2},types(3)))))
17 val =
18     3.2009    3.3896    6.2393
19 >> val(4) = mean(worddata{16}(find(strcmp(worddata{2},types(4)))))
20 val =
21     3.2009    3.3896    6.2393    6.3450
22 >> val(5) = mean(worddata{16}(find(strcmp(worddata{2},types(5)))))
23 val =
24     3.2009    3.3896    6.2393    6.3450    5.1075
25 >> val(6) = mean(worddata{16}(find(strcmp(worddata{2},types(6)))))
26 val =
27     3.2009    3.3896    6.2393    6.3450    5.1075    3.5370
28 >> val(7) = mean(worddata{16}(find(strcmp(worddata{2},types(7)))))
29 val =
30     3.2009    3.3896    6.2393    6.3450    5.1075    3.5370    5.0471
31 >> types'
32 ans =
33   Columns 1 through 5
34     'neg hi ar'    'neg lo ar'    'pos hi ar'    'pos lo ar'    'rel neu'
35   Columns 6 through 7
36     'taboo'    'unrel neu'
37 >> val
38 val =
39     3.2009    3.3896    6.2393    6.3450    5.1075    3.5370    5.0471
```

Question 7

```
 1 >> imagTab = mean(worddata{20}(find(strcmp(worddata{2},'taboo'))))
 2 imagTab =
 3     4.5410
```

```
 4 >> negHiTab = mean(worddata{20}(find(strcmp(worddata{2}, ...
 5 'neg hi ar'))))
 6 negHiTab =
 7     4.5202
 8 >> posHiTab = mean(worddata{20}(find(strcmp(worddata{2}, ...
 9 'pos hi ar'))))
10 posHiTab =
11     4.7183
12 >> negLoTab = mean(worddata{20}(find(strcmp(worddata{2}, ...
13 'neg lo ar'))))
14 negLoTab =
15     4.2839
16 >> posLoTab = mean(worddata{20}(find(strcmp(worddata{2}, ...
17 'pos lo ar'))))
18 posLoTab =
19     5.0804
```

Question 8

```
 1 >> [val,idsImag]=sort(worddata{20}(1:460));
 2 >> TopImag = worddata{1}(idsImag(end:-1:(end-10)))
 3 TopImag =
 4     'cake'
 5     'circle'
 6     'pillow'
 7     'egg'
 8     'pencil'
 9     'snake'
10     'violin'
11     'yellow'
12     'pig'
13     'bunny'
14     'hammer'
15 >> [val,idsLen]=sort(worddata{3}(1:460));
16 >> Len100 = worddata{1}(idsLen(100:110))
17 Len100 =
18     'snob'
19     'chin'
20     'cord'
21     'cork'
22     'farm'
23     'foot'
24     'fork'
25     'item'
26     'knot'
27     'obey'
28     'rain'
```

Question 9

```
1 >> medLetters = median(worddata{3}(1:460))
2 medLetters =
3      5
4 >> medSyllables = median(worddata{4}(1:460))
5 medSyllables =
6      2
```

Chapter 4

Question 1

```
1 >> fid = fopen('JanschewitzB386appB.txt','r');
2 >> formatstring = [ '%s %s' repmat (' %f',1, 19) ];
3 >> worddata=textscan(fid,formatstring,'headerlines',5, ...
4 'delimiter','\t');
5 >> fclose(fid);
6
7 >> types = unique(worddata{2}(1:460));
8 >> imag(1) = mean(worddata{20}(find(strcmp(worddata{2},types(1)))));
9 >> imag(2) = mean(worddata{20}(find(strcmp(worddata{2},types(2)))));
10 >> imag(3) = mean(worddata{20}(find(strcmp(worddata{2},types(3)))));
11 >> imag(4) = mean(worddata{20}(find(strcmp(worddata{2},types(4)))));
12 >> imag(5) = mean(worddata{20}(find(strcmp(worddata{2},types(5)))));
13 >> imag(6) = mean(worddata{20}(find(strcmp(worddata{2},types(6)))));
14 >> imag(7) = mean(worddata{20}(find(strcmp(worddata{2},types(7)))));
15 >> imag
16
17 >> barh(imag)
18 >> set(gca,'YTick',1:7)
19 >> set(gca,'YTickLabel',types)
```

Blank lines were added to improve readability.

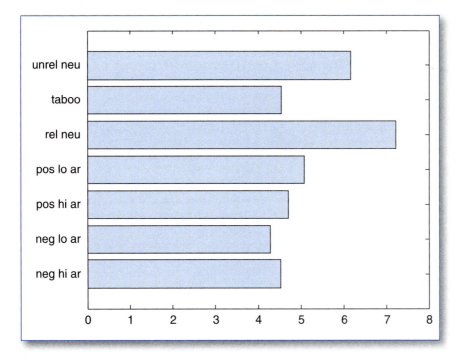

Question 2

```
 1 >> types=unique(worddata{2}(1:460))
 2 >> i=1;
 3 >> mFam(i)=mean(worddata{10}(find(strcmp(worddata{2},types{i}))));
 4 >> stdFam(i)=std(worddata{10}(find(strcmp(worddata{2},types{i}))));
 5 >> mUse(i)=mean(worddata{8}(find(strcmp(worddata{2},types{i}))));
 6 >> stdUse(i)=std(worddata{8}(find(strcmp(worddata{2},types{i}))));
 7 >> nWord(i)=sum(strcmp(worddata{2},types{i}));
 8 >> i=i+1;
 9 >> mFam(i)=mean(worddata{10}(find(strcmp(worddata{2},types{i}))));
10 >> stdFam(i)=std(worddata{10}(find(strcmp(worddata{2},types{i}))));
11 >> mUse(i)=mean(worddata{8}(find(strcmp(worddata{2},types{i}))));
12 >> stdUse(i)=std(worddata{8}(find(strcmp(worddata{2},types{i}))));
13 >> nWord(i)=sum(strcmp(worddata{2},types{i}));
14 >> i=i+1;
15 >> mFam(i)=mean(worddata{10}(find(strcmp(worddata{2},types{i}))));
16 >> stdFam(i)=std(worddata{10}(find(strcmp(worddata{2},types{i}))));
```

(Continued)

(Continued)

```
17 >> mUse(i)=mean(worddata{8}(find(strcmp(worddata{2},types{i}))));
18 >> stdUse(i)=std(worddata{8}(find(strcmp(worddata{2},types{i}))));
19 >> nWord(i)=sum(strcmp(worddata{2},types{i}));
20 >> i=i+1;
21 >> mFam(i)=mean(worddata{10}(find(strcmp(worddata{2},types{i}))));
22 >> stdFam(i)=std(worddata{10}(find(strcmp(worddata{2},types{i}))));
23 >> mUse(i)=mean(worddata{8}(find(strcmp(worddata{2},types{i}))));
24 >> stdUse(i)=std(worddata{8}(find(strcmp(worddata{2},types{i}))));
25 >> nWord(i)=sum(strcmp(worddata{2},types{i}));
26 >> i=i+1;
27 >> mFam(i)=mean(worddata{10}(find(strcmp(worddata{2},types{i}))));
28 >> stdFam(i)=std(worddata{10}(find(strcmp(worddata{2},types{i}))));
29 >> mUse(i)=mean(worddata{8}(find(strcmp(worddata{2},types{i}))));
30 >> stdUse(i)=std(worddata{8}(find(strcmp(worddata{2},types{i}))));
31 >> nWord(i)=sum(strcmp(worddata{2},types{i}));
32 >> i=i+1;
33 >> mFam(i)=mean(worddata{10}(find(strcmp(worddata{2},types{i}))));
34 >> stdFam(i)=std(worddata{10}(find(strcmp(worddata{2},types{i}))));
35 >> mUse(i)=mean(worddata{8}(find(strcmp(worddata{2},types{i}))));
36 >> stdUse(i)=std(worddata{8}(find(strcmp(worddata{2},types{i}))));
37 >> nWord(i)=sum(strcmp(worddata{2},types{i}));
38 >> i=i+1;
39 >> mFam(i)=mean(worddata{10}(find(strcmp(worddata{2},types{i}))));
40 >> stdFam(i)=std(worddata{10}(find(strcmp(worddata{2},types{i}))));
41 >> mUse(i)=mean(worddata{8}(find(strcmp(worddata{2},types{i}))));
42 >> stdUse(i)=std(worddata{8}(find(strcmp(worddata{2},types{i}))));
43 >> nWord(i)=sum(strcmp(worddata{2},types{i}));
44
45 >> mFam
46 >> semFam = stdFam./sqrt(nWord)
47
48 >> mUse
49 >> semUse = stdUse./sqrt(nWord)
50
51 >> bar((1:7)-.2,mFam,'facecolor',imbhex2color('91D2E2'), ...
52 'barwidth',.35)
53 >> hold on
54 >> bar((1:7)+.2,mUse,'facecolor',imbhex2color('E5E5E5'), ...
55 'barwidth',.35)
56 >> errorbar((1:7)-.2,mFam,semFam,'.k','markersize',1)
57 >> errorbar((1:7)+.2,mUse,semUse,'.k','markersize',1)
58 >> axis([0 8 1 9])
59 >> set(gca,'XTick',1:7)
60 >> set(gca,'XTickLabel',types)
61 >> plot([0 8],[1 1],'k')
62 >> legend('Familiarity','Personal Use')
63 >> legend boxoff
```

```
64 >> set(gca,'fontsize',10)
65 >> a=xlabel('Word Type');
66 >> b=ylabel('Mean Rating');
67 >> set(a,'fontsize',14,'fontweight','bold')
68 >> set(b,'fontsize',14,'fontweight','bold')
69 >> set(gca,'TickDir','out')
70 >> box off
71 >> hold off
```

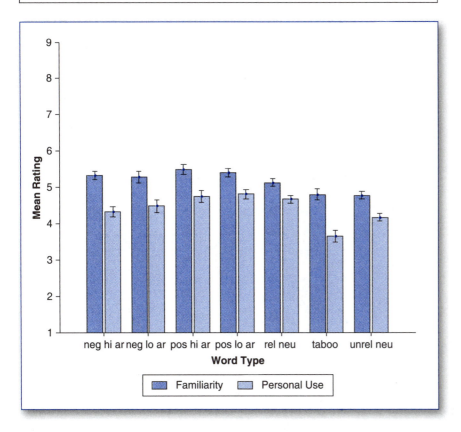

Question 3

```
1 >> types = unique(worddata{2}(1:460));
2 >> aro1 = worddata{18}(find(strcmp(worddata{2},types{1})));
3 >> val1 = worddata{16}(find(strcmp(worddata{2},types{1})));
4 >> aro2 = worddata{18}(find(strcmp(worddata{2},types{2})));
5 >> val2 = worddata{16}(find(strcmp(worddata{2},types{2})));
6 >> aro3 = worddata{18}(find(strcmp(worddata{2},types{3})));
```

(Continued)

(Continued)

```
 7 >> val3 = worddata{16}(find(strcmp(worddata{2},types{3})));
 8 >> aro4 = worddata{18}(find(strcmp(worddata{2},types{4})));
 9 >> val4 = worddata{16}(find(strcmp(worddata{2},types{4})));
10 >> aro5 = worddata{18}(find(strcmp(worddata{2},types{5})));
11 >> val5 = worddata{16}(find(strcmp(worddata{2},types{5})));
12 >> aro6 = worddata{18}(find(strcmp(worddata{2},types{6})));
13 >> val6 = worddata{16}(find(strcmp(worddata{2},types{6})));
14 >> aro7 = worddata{18}(find(strcmp(worddata{2},types{7})));
15 >> val7 = worddata{16}(find(strcmp(worddata{2},types{7})));
16
17 >> scatter(val1,aro1,'vr')
18 >> hold on
19 >> scatter(val2,aro2,'ms')
20 >> scatter(val3,aro3,'^b')
21 >> scatter(val4,aro4,'cd')
22 >> scatter(val5,aro5,'+y')
23 >> scatter(val6,aro6,'xk')
24 >> scatter(val7,aro7,'pg')
25 >> xlabel('Valence')
26 >> ylabel('Arousal')
27 >> axis([1 9 1 9])
28 >> legend(types)
```

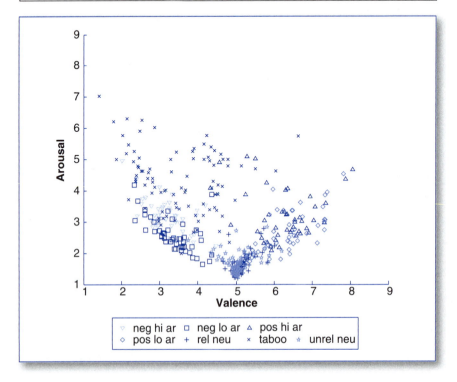

Question 4

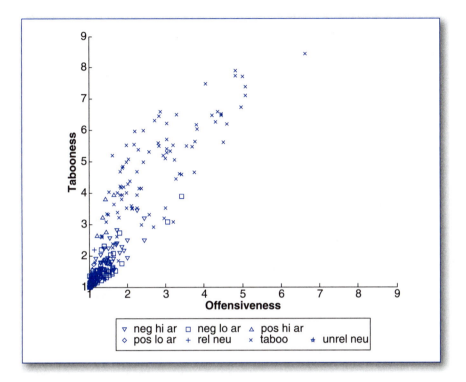

```
 1 >> types=unique(worddata{2}(1:460));
 2 >> tab1 = worddata{14}(find(strcmp(worddata{2},types{1})));
 3 >> off1 = worddata{12}(find(strcmp(worddata{2},types{1})));
 4 >> tab2 = worddata{14}(find(strcmp(worddata{2},types{2})));
 5 >> off2 = worddata{12}(find(strcmp(worddata{2},types{2})));
 6 >> tab3 = worddata{14}(find(strcmp(worddata{2},types{3})));
 7 >> off3 = worddata{12}(find(strcmp(worddata{2},types{3})));
 8 >> tab4 = worddata{14}(find(strcmp(worddata{2},types{4})));
 9 >> off4 = worddata{12}(find(strcmp(worddata{2},types{4})));
10 >> tab5 = worddata{14}(find(strcmp(worddata{2},types{5})));
11 >> off5 = worddata{12}(find(strcmp(worddata{2},types{5})));
12 >> tab6 = worddata{14}(find(strcmp(worddata{2},types{6})));
13 >> off6 = worddata{12}(find(strcmp(worddata{2},types{6})));
14 >> tab7 = worddata{14}(find(strcmp(worddata{2},types{7})));
15 >> off7 = worddata{12}(find(strcmp(worddata{2},types{7})));
16
17 >> scatter(off1,tab1,'vr')
18 >> hold on
19 >> scatter(off2,tab2,'ms')
```

(Continued)

(Continued)

```
20 >> scatter(off3,tab3,'^b')
21 >> scatter(off4,tab4,'cd')
22 >> scatter(off5,tab5,'+y')
23 >> scatter(off6,tab6,'xk')
24 >> scatter(off7,tab7,'pg')
25 >> xlabel('Offensiveness')
26 >> ylabel('Tabooness')
27 >> axis([1 9 1 9])
28 >> legend(types)
```

Question 5

```
 1 >> load data.txt
 2 >> sort(data(:,2))'
 3 ans =
 4    Columns 1 through 10
 5      77     80     81     83     83     83     85     88     89     89
 6    Columns 11 through 20
 7      90     91     92     96     97     99    100    101    103    103
 8    Columns 21 through 30
 9     130    132    132    133    133    133    133    133    135    135
10    Columns 31 through 40
11     137    138    139    139    140    140    140    141    141    144
12 >> HIQ = data(find(data(:,2)>115),2)'
13 HIQ =
14    Columns 1 through 10
15     133    140    139    133    137    138    133    132    141    135
16    Columns 11 through 20
17     140    132    135    139    141    130    133    144    133    140
18 >> LIQ = data(find(data(:,2)<115),2)'
19 LIQ =
20    Columns 1 through 10
21      99     92     89     96     83    100    101     80     83     97
22    Columns 11 through 20
23      91     85    103     77    103     90     83     88     81     89
24 >> errorbar(1,mean(HIQ),mean(HIQ)-min(HIQ),max(HIQ)-mean(HIQ),'.k')
25 >> hold on
26 >> errorbar(2,mean(LIQ),mean(LIQ)-min(LIQ),max(LIQ)-mean(LIQ),'.k')
27 >> xlabel('Group')
28 >> ylabel('IQ Score')
29 >> set(gca,'XTick',1:2)
30 >> set(gca,'XTickLabel',{'High','Low'})
```

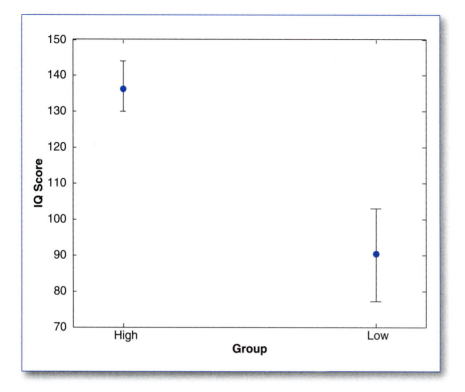

Question 6

```
 1 >> errorbar(1,mean(HIQ),mean(HIQ)-min(HIQ),max(HIQ)-mean(HIQ),'.k')
 2 >> hold on
 3 >> errorbar(2,mean(LIQ),mean(LIQ)-min(LIQ),max(LIQ)-mean(LIQ),'.k')
 4 >> xlabel('Group')
 5 >> ylabel('IQ Score')
 6 >> set(gca,'XTick',1:2)
 7 >> set(gca,'XTickLabel',{'High','Low'})
 8 >> scatter([1 2],[max(HIQ) max(LIQ)],250,'vk', ...
 9    'MarkerFaceColor',[.25 .25 .25])
10 >> scatter([1 2],[min(HIQ) min(LIQ)],250,'^k', ...
11    'MarkerFaceColor',[.25 .25 .25])
12 >> scatter([1 2],[mean(HIQ) mean(LIQ)],250,'ok', ...
13    'MarkerFaceColor',[.75 .75 .75])
14 >> set(gca,'TickDir','out')
```

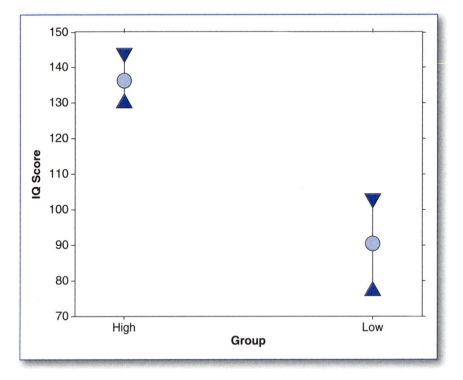

Chapter 5

Question 1

Code:

```
1 fid = fopen('JanschewitzB386appB.txt','r');
2 formatstring = [ '%s %s' repmat(' %f',1,19) ];
3 worddata=textscan(fid,formatstring,'headerlines',5,'delimiter','\t');
4 fclose(fid);
5
6 types=unique(worddata{2}(1:460));
7 for i = 1:length(types)
8     val(i) = mean(worddata{16}(find(strcmp(worddata{2},types(i)))));
9 end
10
11 types
12 val
```

Output:

```
 1 types =
 2     'neg hi ar'
 3     'neg lo ar'
 4     'pos hi ar'
 5     'pos lo ar'
 6     'rel neu'
 7     'taboo'
 8     'unrel neu'
 9 val =
10     3.2009   3.3896   6.2393   6.3450   5.1075   3.5370   5.0471
```

Question 2

Code:

```
 1 types=unique(worddata{2}(1:460))
 2
 3 for i=1:length(types)
 4     mFam(i)=mean(worddata{10}(find(strcmp(worddata{2},types{i}))));
 5     stdFam(i)=std(worddata{10}(find(strcmp(worddata{2},types{i}))));
 6
 7     mUse(i)=mean(worddata{8}(find(strcmp(worddata{2},types{i}))));
 8     stdUse(i)=std(worddata{8}(find(strcmp(worddata{2},types{i}))));
 9
10   nWord(i)=sum(strcmp(worddata{2},types{i}));
11 end
12
13 mFam
14 semFam = stdFam./sqrt(nWord)
15
16 mUse
17 semUse = stdUse./sqrt(nWord)
18
19 bar((1:7)-.2,mFam,'facecolor',imbhex2color('91D2E2'),'barwidth',.35)
20 hold on
21 bar((1:7)+.2,mUse,'facecolor',imbhex2color('E5E5E5'),'barwidth',.35)
22 errorbar((1:7)-.2,mFam,semFam,'.k','markersize',1)
23 errorbar((1:7)+.2,mUse,semUse,'.k','markersize',1)
24
25 axis([0 8 1 9])
26 set(gca,'XTick',1:7)
27 set(gca,'XTickLabel',types)
```

(Continued)

(Continued)

```
28 plot([0 8],[1 1],'k')
29 legend('Familiarity','Personal Use')
30 legend boxoff
31 set(gca,'fontsize',10)
32 a=xlabel('Word Type');
33 b=ylabel('Mean Rating');
34 set(a,'fontsize',14,'fontweight','bold')
35 set(b,'fontsize',14,'fontweight','bold')
36 set(gca,'TickDir','out')
37 box off
38 hold off
```

Output:

```
 1 types =
 2     'neg hi ar'
 3     'neg lo ar'
 4     'pos hi ar'
 5     'pos lo ar'
 6     'rel neu'
 7     'taboo'
 8     'unrel neu'
 9 mFam =
10     5.3176    5.2763    5.4902    5.3974    5.1266    4.7927    4.7752
11 semFam =
12     0.1154    0.1598    0.1423    0.1124    0.0982    0.1522    0.1035
13 mUse =
14     4.3250    4.4787    4.7383    4.8080    4.6620    3.6446    4.1699
15 semUse =
16     0.1341    0.1782    0.1693    0.1320    0.1156    0.1578    0.1136
```

The figure produced is the same as in Chapter 4, Question 2.

Question 3

```
1 for sub = 1:20
2     load(sprintf('subject4%02.of',sub))
3     ERdir(sub,:) = [sub mean(ER(find(ST==1))) mean(ER(find(ST==0)))];
4 end
```

Question 4

```
1 function nOccur = freq(x)
2
3 vals = unique(x);
4
5 for i = 1:length(vals)
6     nOccur(i,:) = [ vals(i) sum(x==vals(i)) ];
7 end
```

Question 5

```
1 >> D(find(trialnum==1))
2 ans =
3     0.5000    2.0000    0.5000    1.0000    2.0000
4 >> Dpen(find(trialnum==1))
5 ans =
6     1.5000         0         0         0         0
```

Chapter 6

Question 1

```
1 fid = fopen('JanschewitzB386appB.txt','r');
2 formatstring = [ '%s %s' repmat (' %f',1,19) ];
3 'worddata=textscan(fid,formatstring,'headerlines',5,'delimiter','\t');
4 fclose(fid);
```

Question 2

```
1 scatter(worddata{10}(1:460),worddata{8}(1:460))
```

Error: Both inputs need to have the same number of rows. worddata
itself has a few "extra" rows at the end.

Question 3

```
1 imagTab = mean(worddata{20}(find(strcmp(worddata{2},'taboo'))))
```

Error: Missing brackets, both after `strcmp` and one at the end. The comma after `strcmp` also shouldn't be there.

Question 4

```
1 types=unique(worddata{2}(1:460))
```

Error: `worddata` is a cell array of several matrices; you can't combine the two dimensions.

Question 5

```
1 % find numbers divisible by 3 within certain range
2 numbers = 277:300;
3 div3 = numbers(find(mod(numbers,3)==0));
```

Chapter 7

Question 1

Code:

```
1 for sub = 1:20
2     load(sprintf('subject4%02.0f',sub))
3     ERsub(sub,:) = [ sub mean(ER(find(D==1))) mean(ER(find(D==2))) ];
4 End
5 [h,p,ci,stat]=ttest(ERsub(:,2),ERsub(:,3))
```

Output:

```
1 h =
2     1
3 p =
4     0.0036
5 ci =
6     0.0111
7     0.0488
8 stat =
```

```
 9       tstat: 3.3230
10          df: 19
11          sd: 0.0403
```

Question 2

Code:

```
1 for sub = 1:20
2     load(sprintf('subject4%02.0f',sub))
3     ERdir(sub,:) = [sub mean(ER(find(ST==1))) mean(ER(find(ST==0)))];
4 end
5
6 [h,p,ci,stat]=ttest(ERdir(:,2),ERdir(:,3))
```

Output:

```
 1 h =
 2       0
 3 p =
 4      0.0579
 5 ci =
 6     -0.0617
 7      0.0011
 8 stat =
 9       tstat: -2.0186
10          df: 19
11          sd: 0.0671
```

Question 3

Code:

```
1 fid = fopen('JanschewitzB386appB.txt','r');
2 formatstring = [ '%s %s' repmat (' %f'1,19) ];
3 'worddata=textscan(fid,formatstring,'headerlines',5,'delimiter','\t');
4 fclose(fid);
5
6 offNegHi = worddata{12}(find(strcmp(worddata{2},'neg hi ar')));
7 offPosHi = worddata{12}(find(strcmp(worddata{2},'pos hi ar')));
8
9 [h,p,ci,stat]=ttest2(offNegHi,offPosHi)
```

Output:

```
 1  h =
 2       1
 3  p =
 4       7.5106e-10
 5  ci =
 6       0.2779
 7       0.5034
 8  stat =
 9       tstat: 6.8858
10          df: 90
11          sd: 0.2721
```

Question 4

Code:

```
1  fam = worddata{10}(1:460);
2  use = worddata{8}(1:460);
3  [r,p] = corr(fam,use)
```

Output:

```
1  r =
2       0.9325
3  p =
4     9.5203e-205
```

Question 5

```
 1  >> val = worddata{16}(1:460);
 2  >> aro = worddata{18(1:460);
 3  >> [r,p] = corr(val,aro)
 4  r =
 5      -0.3766
 6  p =
 7      6.0231e-17
 8  >> [h,p,jbstat] = jbtest(val)
 9  h =
10       0
11  p =
12       0.1114
```

```
13 jbstat =
14     4.0923
15 >> [h,p,jbstat] = jbtest(aro)
16 Warning: P is less than the smallest tabulated value, returning 0.001.
17 > In jbtest at 143
18 h =
19     1
20 p =
21     1.0000e-03
22 jbstat =
23     61.5009
24 >> [rho,p] = corr(val,aro,'type','spearman')
25 rho =
26    -0.3435
27 p =
28     3.4778e-14
```

Also see Figure 4.7 (p. 78) as well as Chapter 4, Question 3.

Question 6

Output:

```
 1 >> freq2(worddata{2}(1:460))
 2 ans =
 3     'neg hi ar'    [46]
 4     'neg lo ar'    [46]
 5     'pos hi ar'    [46]
 6     'pos lo ar'    [46]
 7     'rel neu'      [92]
 8     'taboo'        [92]
 9     'unrel neu'    [92]
10 >> freq2(blocknum)
11 ans =
12     1    247
13     2    147
14     3    347
15     4    239
16     5    150
```

This code is a bit more complicated than what you've done previously, but we're trying to get you to push your boundaries a bit!

Code:

```
1 function nOccur = freq2(x)
2
3 vals = unique(x);
4
5 for i = 1:length(vals)
6     if iscell(vals(i))
7         nOccur{i,:} = [ vals(i) sum(strcmp(x,vals(i))) ];
8     else
9         nOccur{i,:} = [ vals(i) sum(x==vals(i)) ];
10     end
11 end
12
13 nOccur = [nOccur{:}];
14 nOccur = reshape(nOccur,2,length(nOccur)/2)';
```

Chapter 8

As mentioned previously, there are often many ways to arrive at the same solution, and this is particularly the case given these questions provided less direction. Given below are simply the best answers I could come up with. If you are interested in seeing if your answer is more efficient than my own, feel free to use the optimization methods covered in Chapter 6.

8.1

Question 1

```
1 >> load subject101
2 >> EReasy = mean(ER(find(Anum==60)))
3 EReasy =
4      0.0864
5 >> ERdiff = mean(ER(find(Anum==53)))
6 ERdiff =
7      0.3083
```

Question 2

Easy trials:

```
 1 >> EReasyCond(1) = mean(ER(find(Anum==60 & D==.5 & Dpen==0)))
 2 EReasyCond =
 3      0.1220
 4 >> EReasyCond(2) = mean(ER(find(Anum==60 & D==1 & Dpen==0)))
 5 EReasyCond =
 6      0.1220     0.0833
 7 >> EReasyCond(3) = mean(ER(find(Anum==60 & D==2 & Dpen==0)))
 8 EReasyCond =
 9      0.1220     0.0833     0.0707
10 >> EReasyCond(4) = mean(ER(find(Anum==60 & D==.5 & Dpen==1.5)))
11 EReasyCond =
12      0.1220     0.0833     0.0707     0.0636
```

Difficult trials:

```
1 ERdiffCond(1) = mean(ER(find(Anum==53 & D==.5 & Dpen==0)));
2 ERdiffCond(2) = mean(ER(find(Anum==53 & D==1 & Dpen==0)));
3 ERdiffCond(3) = mean(ER(find(Anum==53 & D==2 & Dpen==0)));
4 ERdiffCond(4) = mean(ER(find(Anum==53 & D==.5 & Dpen==1.5)));
5 ERdiffCond
```

Output:

```
1 ERdiffCond =
2    0.3822     0.2516     0.3175     0.2364
```

Question 3

Code:

```
1 easy = 60;
2 diff = 53;
3 condD = [ .5 1 2 .5 ];
4 condDpen = [ 0 0 0 1.5 ];
5
6 for sub = 1:20
```

(Continued)

(Continued)

```
 7     load(sprintf('subject%.0f',sub+100))
 8     for cond = 1:4
 9         EReasyCond(sub,cond) = mean(ER(find(Anum==easy & ...
10             D==condD(cond) & Dpen==condDpen(cond))));
11         ERdiffCond(sub,cond) = mean(ER(find(Anum==diff & ...
12             D==condD(cond) & Dpen==condDpen(cond))));
13         RTeasyCond(sub,cond) = mean(RT(find(Anum==easy & ...
14             D==condD(cond) & Dpen==condDpen(cond))));
15         RTdiffCond(sub,cond) = mean(RT(find(Anum==diff & ...
16             D==condD(cond) & Dpen==condDpen(cond))));
17     end
18 end
19
20 EReasyCond
21 ERdiffCond
22 RTeasyCond
23 RTdiffCond
```

Note that the . . . is only needed here as the code would not otherwise fit on the printed page.

Output:

```
 1 EReasyCond =
 2      0.1220    0.0833    0.0707    0.0636
 3      0.4505    0.0705    0.0444    0.0706
 4      0.0265    0.0204    0.0333    0.0103
 5      0.1700    0.0982    0.1244    0.0962
 6      0.0311    0.0559    0.0214    0.0563
 7      ...
 8 ERdiffCond =
 9      0.3822    0.2516    0.3175    0.2364
10      0.4846    0.4643    0.3701    0.3203
11      0.4396    0.2326    0.2360    0.1667
12      0.4000    0.3087    0.2626    0.2789
13      0.3043    0.2042    0.2744    0.2397
14      ...
15 RTeasyCond =
16      0.4415    0.4329    0.4384    0.4176
17      0.0262    0.5384    0.6740    0.8051
```

```
18      0.6755      0.5966      0.6591      0.5064
19      0.4459      0.4750      0.4960      0.5076
20      0.5629      0.4945      0.5735      0.5385
21      ...
22 RTdiffCond =
23      0.4254      0.5113      0.5560      0.5968
24      0.0251      0.0718      1.1303      0.9007
25      0.2372      0.8304      0.9576      0.7948
26      0.4778      0.6162      0.7053      0.7104
27      0.7980      0.6912      0.9464      0.7844
28      ...
```

Question 4

Code:

```
 1 easy = 60;
 2 diff = 53;
 3 condD = [ .5 1 2 .5 ];
 4 condDpen = [ 0 0 0 1.5 ];
 5
 6 for sub = 1:20
 7     load(sprintf('subject%.0f',sub+100))
 8     for cond = 1:4
 9         EReasyCond(sub,cond) = mean(ER(find(Anum==easy & ...
10             D==condD(cond) & Dpen==condDpen(cond))));
11         ERdiffCond(sub,cond) = mean(ER(find(Anum==diff & ...
12             D==condD(cond) & Dpen==condDpen(cond))));
13         RTeasyCond(sub,cond) = mean(RT(find(Anum==easy & ...
14             D==condD(cond) & Dpen==condDpen(cond) & ER==0)));
15         RTdiffCond(sub,cond) = mean(RT(find(Anum==diff & ...
16             D==condD(cond) & Dpen==condDpen(cond) & ER==0)));
17     end
18 end
19
20
21 EReasyCond
22 ERdiffCond
23 RTeasyCond
24 RTdiffCond
```

Output:

```
 1 EReasyCond =
 2     0.1220    0.0833    0.0707    0.0636
 3     0.4505    0.0705    0.0444    0.0706
 4     0.0265    0.0204    0.0333    0.0103
 5     0.1700    0.0982    0.1244    0.0962
 6     0.0311    0.0559    0.0214    0.0563
 7     ...
 8 ERdiffCond =
 9     0.3822    0.2516    0.3175    0.2364
10     0.4846    0.4643    0.3701    0.3203
11     0.4396    0.2326    0.2360    0.1667
12     0.4000    0.3087    0.2626    0.2789
13     0.3043    0.2042    0.2744    0.2397
14     ...
15 RTeasyCond =
16     0.4406    0.4339    0.4393    0.4195
17     0.0307    0.5391    0.6671    0.7896
18     0.6625    0.5960    0.6481    0.5064
19     0.4498    0.4785    0.5028    0.5113
20     0.5544    0.4883    0.5721    0.5347
21     ...
22 RTdiffCond =
23     0.4526    0.4975    0.5576    0.5911
24     0.0241    0.0816    1.1053    0.8628
25     0.2621    0.7833    0.8949    0.7566
26     0.4968    0.6235    0.6951    0.7134
27     0.7940    0.6926    0.9112    0.7439
28     ...
```

Question 5

Code:

```
1 mEReasyCond = mean(EReasyCond)
2 mERdiffCond = mean(ERdiffCond)
3
4 semEReasyCond = std(EReasyCond)/sqrt(20)
5 semERdiffCond = std(ERdiffCond)/sqrt(20)
```

Output:

```
1 mEReasyCond =
2      0.1362        0.0624        0.0494        0.0445
3 mERdiffCond =
4      0.3242        0.3122        0.2661        0.2422
5 semEReasyCond =
6      0.0344        0.0127        0.0085        0.0046
7 semERdiffCond =
8      0.0221        0.0212        0.0129        0.0088
```

Question 6

```
 1 posEasy = [1:4]-.2;
 2 posDiff = [1:4]+.2;
 3
 4 figure
 5 hold on
 6 bar(posEasy,mEReasyCond,'barwidth',.35,'facecolor',[.5 .5 .7]);
 7 bar(posDiff,mERdiffCond,'barwidth',.35,'facecolor',[.5 .5 .3]);
 8
 9 legend('Easy','Difficult')
10 legend boxoff
11
12 errorbar(posEasy,mEReasyCond,semEReasyCond,'.k');
13 errorbar(posDiff,mERdiffCond,semERdiffCond,'.k');
14
15 axis([.4 4.5 0 .4])
16
17 xlabel('Delay Condition')
18 ylabel('Error Rate')
19
20 set(gca,'XTick',1:4);
21 set(gca,'XTickLabel',{'.5' '1' '2' '.5+1.5'});
22 set(gca,'YTick',0:.05:.4);
23
24 set(gca,'TickDir','out');
25
26 orient landscape
27 print('-dpdf','meanER.pdf')
```

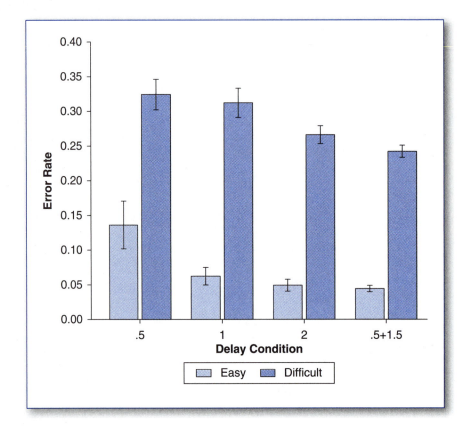

Question 7

```
 1 posEasy = [1:4]-.2;
 2 posDiff = [1:4]+.2;
 3
 4 figure
 5 set(gca,'fontsize',26);
 6 set(gca,'linewidth',2);
 7 hold on
 8 bar(posEasy,mEReasyCond,'barwidth',.35,'facecolor',[.5 .5 .7], ...
 9     'linewidth',2);
10 bar(posDiff,mERdiffCond,'barwidth',.35,'facecolor',[.5 .5 .3], ...
11     'linewidth',2);
12 legend('Easy','Difficult')
13 legend boxoff
14
15 errorbar(posEasy,mEReasyCond,semEReasyCond,'.k','linewidth',2);
16 errorbar(posDiff,mERdiffCond,semERdiffCond,'.k','linewidth',2);
```

```
17
18 axis([.4 4.5 0 .4])
19 h=xlabel('Delay Condition');
20 set(h,'fontweight','bold');
21 h=ylabel('Error Rate');
22 set(h,'fontweight','bold');
23
24 set(gca,'XTick',1:4);
25 set(gca,'XTickLabel',{'.5' '1' '2' '.5+1.5'});
26 ys = 0:.05:.4;
27 set(gca,'YTick',ys);
28 for i = 1:length(ys)
29     ys_text{i} = sprintf('%.02f',ys(i));
30 end
31 set(gca,'YTickLabel',ys_text);
32 set(gca,'TickDir','out');
33
34 orient landscape
35 print('-dpdf','meanER2.pdf')
```

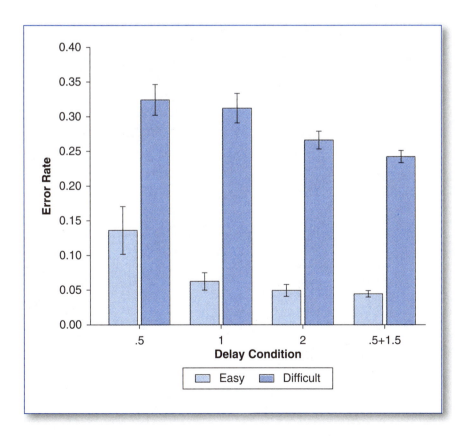

8.2

Question 1

```
1 nToss = 100;
2
3 for i = 1:nToss
4     outcome(i) = round(rand);
5 end
```

Question 2

```
1 nToss = 100;
2 outcome = round(rand(1,nToss));
```

Question 3

```
1 >> nHeads = sum(outcome==1)
2 nHeads =
3     44
4 >> nTails = sum(outcome==0)
5 nTails =
6     56
```

If you want, you could have used the `freq` function you wrote previously.

Note that the output from your MATLAB will differ as this exercise is based on random numbers.

Question 4

```
1 function rmean = runningmean(x,N)
2 % x = list of values
3 % N = window to compute running means across
4 % Output: rmean = running mean(same length as x)
5 for i = 1:length(x)
6     if i < N
7         rmean(i) = NaN;
```

```
 8      else
 9            rmean(i) = mean(x( (i-N):i ));
10      end
11 end
```

Question 5

```
 1 >> nToss = 100;
 2 >> outcome = round(ceil(rand(1,nToss)*6));
 3 >> for d = 1:6
 4 cSide(d) = sum(outcome==d);
 5 end
 6 >> cSide
 7 cSide =
 8      17      14      15      15      21      18
 9 >> [ 1:6; cSide ]
10 ans =
11      1      2      3      4      5      6
12      17     14     15     15     21     18
```

Again, you could have used the freq function you wrote previously.

Question 6

```
 1 >> nToss = 100;
 2 >> nSide = 20;
 3 >> outcome = round(ceil(rand(1,nToss)*nSide));
 4 >> for d = 1:nSide
 5 cSide(d) = sum(outcome==d);
 6 end
 7 >> [ 1:nSide; cSide ]
 8 ans =
 9    Columns 1 through 10
10      1      2      3      4      5      6      7      8      9     10
11      4      7      7      8      5      4      3      6      7      5
12    Columns 11 through 20
13     11     12     13     14     15     16     17     18     19     20
14      7      2      5      3      3      6      5      3      7      3
```

Question 7

```
 1 >> nToss = 100;
 2 >> nSide = 20;
 3 >> randmat = rand(nSide,nToss);
 4 >> [j,outcome] = max(randmat);
 5 >> for d = 1:nSide
 6 cSide(d) = sum(outcome==d);
 7 end
 8 >> [ 1:nSide; cSide ]
 9 ans =
10    Columns 1 through 10
11       1      2      3      4      5      6      7      8      9     10
12       4      6      3      3      8      4      8      2      7      8
13    Columns 11 through 20
14      11     12     13     14     15     16     17     18     19     20
15       2      9      5      1      7      6      2      7      4      4
```

8.3

Question 1

```
1 fid = fopen('BristolNorms30-08-05.txt','r');
2 formatstring = [ '%s' repmat(' %f',1,9) ];
3 worddata=textscan(fid,formatstring,'headerlines',2,'delimiter','\t');
4 fclose(fid);
```

Question 2

```
1 img = worddata{4};
2 fam = worddata{5};
3 scatter(img,fam)
4 xlabel('Imageability')
5 ylabel('Familiarity')
6 axis([ 100 700 100 700 ])
```

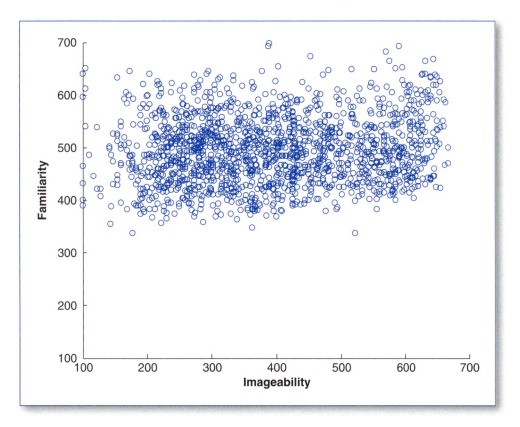

Question 3

Code:

```
1  img = worddata{4};
2  aoa = worddata{2};
3  [r,p] = corr(img,aoa)
```

Output:

```
1  r =
2     -0.5215
3  p =
4.   3.7625e-107
```

Question 4

Code:

```
1 aoa = worddata{2};
2 lenL = worddata{6};
3 lenS = worddata{7};
4 lenP = worddata{8};
5
6 [rL,p] = corr(aoa,lenL)
7 [rS,p] = corr(aoa,lenS)
8 [rP,p] = corr(aoa,lenP)
```

Output:

```
1 rL =
2      0.2858
3 p =
4      4.5785e-30
5 rS =
6      0.3371
7 p =
8      7.2678e-42
9 rP =
10      0.3303
11 p =
12      3.5656e-40
```

Question 5

```
1 >> aoa = worddata{2};
2 >> [val,id]=max(aoa)
3 val =
4      12.6000
5 id =
6      668
7 >> worddata{1}(id)
8 ans =
9      'hernia'
10 >> [val,id]=min(aoa)
11 val =
12      2.1000
13 id =
14      863
15 >> worddata{1}(id)
16 ans =
17      'mummy'
```

Question 6

```
 1 >> img = worddata{4};
 2 >> [vals,ids] = sort(img);
 3 >> vals(1:10)
 4 ans =
 5     100
 6     100
 7     100
 8     100
 9     100
10     100
11     105
12     105
13     105
14     111
15 >> % low imageability
16 >> worddata{1}(ids(1:10))
17 ans =
18     'affect'
19     'dogma'
20     'entail'
21     'ever'
22     'overt'
23     'quantum'
24     'become'
25     'innate'
26     'other'
27     'output'
28 >> vals((end:-1:(end-10)))
29 ans =
30     668
31     668
32     664
33     662
34     661
35     660
36     659
37     655
38     655
39     655
40     654
41 >> % high imageability
42 >> worddata{1}(ids((end:-1:(end-10))))
43 ans =
44     'hammer'
```

(Continued)

(Continued)

```
45      'bride'
46      'bath'
47      'rainbow'
48      'dress'
49      'beach'
50      'sausage'
51      'trouser'
52      'tractor'
53      'leaf'
54      'nurse'
```

Question 7

```
1 >> aoa = worddata{2};
2 >> [vals,ids] = sort(aoa);
3 >> ImagLaoa = worddata{4}(ids(1:100));
4 >> ImagHaoa = worddata{4}(ids(end:-1:(end-100)));
5 >> [h,p,ci,stat] = ttest2(ImagLaoa,ImagHaoa)
6 h =
7        1
8 p =
9      3.1280e-40
10 ci =
11     227.6953
12     287.9722
13 stat =
14      tstat: 16.8700
15         df: 199
16         sd: 108.3394
```

8.4

Question 1

```
1 fid = fopen('expansion.txt','r');
2 formatstring = '%s %f %f %f';
3 searches = textscan(fid,formatstring,'headerlines',1, ...
4 'delimiter','\t');
5 fclose(fid);
```

Question 2

Code:

```
1  rowsL = strcmp(searches{1},'Landmark');
2  birdsL = unique(searches{2}(find(rowsL)));
3
4  totalSearches = [];
5  for b = 1:length(birdsL)
6      totalSearches(b) = sum(searches{4}(find( ...
7      searches{2} == birdsL(b))));
8  end
9
10 propSearchL = [];
11 for b = 1:length(birdsL)
12     for g = 1:100
13         propSearchL(b,g) = searches{4}(find( ...
14         searches{2} == birdsL(b) & searches{3} == g))/totalSearches(b);
15     end
16 end
17
18 mSearchL = mean(propSearchL);
19 mSearchL
20
21 sum(mSearchL)
```

Output:

```
1  mSearchL =
2    Columns 1 through 5
3         0          0     0.0016          0     0.0049
4    Columns 6 through 10
5      0.0091     0.0154     0.0089     0.0016          0
6    Columns 11 through 15
7         0     0.0060     0.0118     0.0242     0.0202
8    Columns 16 through 20
9      0.0183     0.0187     0.0203     0.0052          0
10   ...
11 ans =
12     1.0000
```

Question 3

```
 1 figure
 2 hold on
 3
 4 axis([0 10 0 10])
 5 set(gca,'XTick',[])
 6 set(gca,'YTick',[])
 7
 8 grid = 0;
 9
10 for g1 = 1:10
11     for g2 = 1:10
12         grid = grid + 1;
13         if mSearchL(grid) > 0
14             scatter(g2-.5,g1-.5,mSearchL(grid)*2500,'sk', ...
15                 'MarkerFaceColor','k')
16         end
17     end
18 end
19
20 box on
```

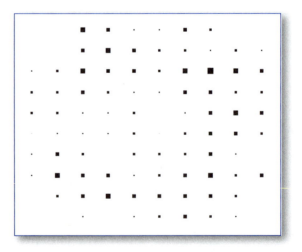

Question 4

```
1 fp = fillPage(gcf, 'margins', [0 0 0 0], 'papersize', [6 6]);
2 print('2dpeck_landmark.pdf','-dpdf')
```

Question 5

```
 1 groupName = {'Landmark' 'Wall'};
 2
 3 fid = fopen('expansion.txt','r');
 4 formatstring = '%s %f %f %f';
 5 searches = textscan(fid,formatstring,'headerlines',1, ...
 6 'delimiter','\t');
 7 fclose(fid);
 8
 9 for group = 1:2
10     clear rows birds mSearch
11     rows = strcmp(searches{1},groupName{group});
12     birds = unique(searches{2}(find(rows)));
13     totalSearches = [];
14     for b = 1:length(birds)
15         totalSearches(b) = sum(searches{4}( ...
16         find(searches{2} == birds(b))));
17     end
18
19     propSearch = [];
20     for b = 1:length(birds)
21         for g = 1:100
22             propSearch(b,g) = searches{4}(find( ...
23                 searches{2} == birds(b) & searches{3} == g))/ ...
24                 totalSearches(b);
25         end
26     end
27     mSearch = mean(propSearch);
28
```

(Continued)

(Continued)

```
29      figure
30      hold on
31      axis([0 10 0 10])
32      set(gca,'XTick',[])
33      set(gca,'YTick',[])
34
35      grid = 0;
36      for g1 = 1:10
37          for g2 = 1:10
38              grid = grid + 1;
39              if mSearch(grid) > 0
40                  scatter(g2-.5,g1-.5,mSearch(grid)*2500,'sk', ...
41                      'MarkerFaceColor','k')
42              end
43          end
44      end
45
46      box on
47      fp = fillPage(gcf, 'margins', [0 0 0 0], 'papersize', [6 6]);
48      print(sprintf('2dpeck_%s.pdf',groupName{group}),'-dpdf')
49      close all
50
51 end
```

Figure for the Wall group:

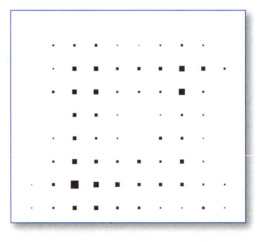

Question 6

```
1 figure
2 hold on
3
4 set(gca,'LineWidth',3)
```

```
 5
 6 for i = 1:10
 7     plot([0 10], [i i],'k','LineWidth',3)
 8     plot([i i], [0 10],'k','LineWidth',3)
 9 end
10
11 axis([0 10 0 10])
12 set(gca,'XTick',[])
13 set(gca,'YTick',[])
14
15 grid = 0;
16 for g1 = 1:10
17     for g2 = 1:10
18         grid = grid + 1;
19         text(g2-.5,g1-.5,sprintf('%.0f',grid), ...
20             'HorizontalAlignment','center', ...
21             'FontSize',16);
22     end
23 end
24
25 box on
26 fp = fillPage(gcf, 'margins', [0 0 0 0], 'papersize', [6 6]);
27 print('grid_labelled.pdf','-dpdf')
```

8.5

Question 1

```
1 >> img = imread('images/0001.jpg');
2 >> imshow(img)
```

Source: Cerf et al. (2007).

Question 2

```
1 >> img = imread('images/0001.jpg');
2 >> load annotations
3 >> an{1}.object{1}
4 ans =
5     mask: [18916x1 double]
6     name: 'face'
7 >> imgFace = img;
8 >> imgFace(an{1}.object{1}.mask) = 0;
9 >> imshow(imgFace)
```

Source: Cerf et al. (2007).

Question 3

Source: Cerf et al. (2007).

Source: Cerf et al. (2007).

```
 1 function [] = fixplot(imgID)
 2
 3 img = imread(sprintf('images/%04.of.jpg',imgID));
 4 load fixations
 5
 6 figure
 7 imshow(img)
 8 hold on
 9
10 for sub = 1:length(sbj)
11     for fix = 1:length(sbj{sub}.scan{imgID}.fix_x)
12         x = sbj{sub}.scan{imgID}.fix_x(fix);
13         y = sbj{sub}.scan{imgID}.fix_y(fix);
14         dur = sbj{sub}.scan{imgID}.fix_duration(fix);
15         scatter(x,y,dur,'ob','LineWidth',3,'MarkerFaceColor','c');
16     end
17 end
18
19 fp = fillPage(gcf, 'margins', [0 0 0 0], 'papersize', ...
20     [size(img,2)/100 size(img,1)/100]);
21 print(sprintf('eyetrack_%o4.0f.pdf',imgID),'-dpdf')
22 close
```

Question 4

```
 1 function [] = eyeplot(imgID)
 2
 3 img = imread(sprintf('images/%04.0f.jpg',imgID));
 4 load fixations
 5
 6 eyeMap = zeros(size(img,1),size(img,2));
 7 for sub = 1:length(sbj)
 8     %sub
 9     for i = 1:length(sbj{sub}.scan{imgID}.scan_x)
10         x = ceil(sbj{sub}.scan{imgID}.scan_x(i));
11         y = ceil(sbj{sub}.scan{imgID}.scan_y(i));
12         if x > 1 & y > 1
13             % exclude positions that are off-screne
14             eyeMap(y,x) = eyeMap(y,x) + 1;
15         end
16     end
17 end
18
19 % change to proportions
20 eyeMap = eyeMap ./ sum(sum(eyeMap));
21
22 % smooth eyeMap with a Guassian Kernel
23 kern1d = normpdf(-10:10,0,5);
24 kern2d = kern1d'*kern1d*10;
25 eyeMapSmooth = conv2(eyeMap,kern2d,'same');
26
27 figure
28 subplot(1,2,1)
29 imshow(img)
30
31 subplot(1,2,2)
32 imshow(eyeMapSmooth*255)
33 colormap(jet)
34
35 fp = fillPage(gcf, 'margins', [0 0 0 0], 'papersize', ...
36     [size(img,2)/100*2 size(img,1)/100]);
37 print(sprintf('eyeplot_%04.0f.pdf',imgID),'-dpdf')
38 close
```

Source: Cerf et al. (2007).

Question 5

```
1 function [] = eyetop(imgID)
2
3 img = imread(sprintf('images/%04.0f.jpg',imgID));
4 load fixations
5
6 eyeMap = zeros(size(img,1),size(img,2));
7 for sub = 1:length(sbj)
8     for i = 1:length(sbj{sub}.scan{imgID}.scan_x)
9         x = ceil(sbj{sub}.scan{imgID}.scan_x(i));
10         y = ceil(sbj{sub}.scan{imgID}.scan_y(i));
11         if x > 1 &  y > 1
12             % exclude positions that are off-screne
13             eyeMap(y,x) = eyeMap(y,x) + 1;
14         end
15     end
16 end
```

(Continued)

(Continued)

```
17
18 % change to proportions
19 eyeMap = eyeMap ./ sum(sum(eyeMap));
20
21 % smooth eyeMap with a Guassian kernel
22 kern1d = normpdf(-10:10,0,5);
23 kern2d = kern1d'*kern1d*10;
24 eyeMapSmooth = conv2(eyeMap,kern2d,'same');
25
26 % average the image and eyeMap
27 imgCombined(:,:,:,1) = img;
28 imgCombined(:,:,2,2) = eyeMapSmooth./max(max(eyeMapSmooth))*255*4;
29 imgCombined = uint8(mean(imgCombined,4));
30
31 figure
32 imshow(imgCombined)
33 imwrite(imgCombined,sprintf('eyetop_%04.0f.jpg',imgID))
```

Source: Cerf et al. (2007).

Source: Cerf et al. (2007).

Question 6

```
1  img = imread('images/0001.jpg');
2
3  img256 = randblock(img,[256 256 3]);
4  imshow(img256)
5  imwrite(img256,'0001_256.jpg')
6  close
7
8  img64 = randblock(img,[64 64 3]);
9  imshow(img64)
10 imwrite(img64,'0001_064.jpg')
11 close
12
13 img16 = randblock(img,[16 16 3]);
14 imshow(img16)
15 imwrite(img16,'0001_016.jpg')
16 close
17
18 img1 = randblock(img,[1 1 3]);
19 imshow(img1)
20 imwrite(img1,'0001_001.jpg')
21 close
```

Note that your images will be somewhat different as randblocks is based on randomization.

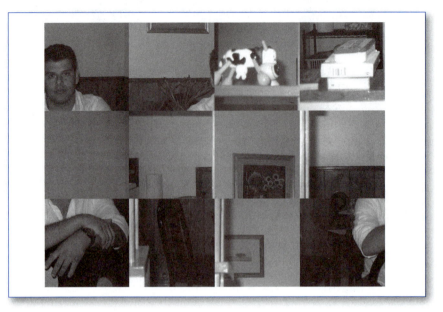

Source: Adapted from Cerf et al. (2007).

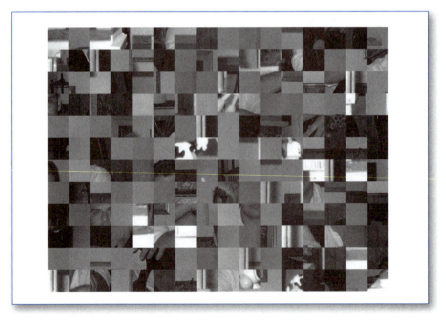

Source: Adapted from Cerf et al. (2007).

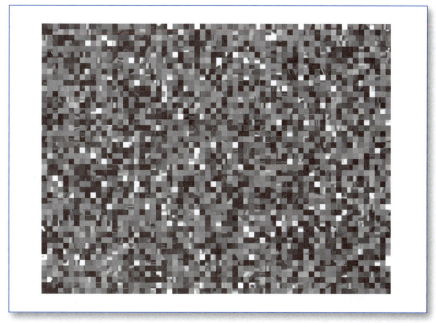

Source: Adapted from Cerf et al. (2007).

Source: Adapted from Cerf et al. (2007).

8.6

Question 1

Code:

```
1 nTrials = 48;
2 nCond = 4;
3
4 seq = repmat(1:nCond,1,nTrials/nCond);
5
6 passed = 0;
7 nTry = 0;
8 while passed == 0
9     seq = seq(randperm(nTrials));
10    passed = 1;
11
12    i = 1;
13    while i < nTrials-2
14      if seq(i) == seq(i+1)
15          if seq(i+1) == seq(i+2)
16              passed = 0;
17          end
18      end
19      i = i + 1;
20    end
21    nTry = nTry + 1;
22 end
23
24 seq
25 nTry
```

Output:

```
1 seq =
2   Columns 1 through 8
3      1     2     3     4     4     1     4     2
4   Columns 9 through 16
5      1     3     4     4     3     2     3     1
6   Columns 17 through 24
7      2     3     1     2     1     3     3     2
8   Columns 25 through 32
9      2     4     2     4     4     1     3     3
10  Columns 33 through 40
```

```
11     2    4    1    1    3    1    2    2
12   Columns 41 through 48
13     3    4    1    4    3    1    2    4
14 nTry =
15     6
```

Question 2

Code:

```
 1 nTrials = 48;
 2 nCond = 4;
 3 ITIlist = [ 1 2 ];
 4
 5 ITIcond = [];
 6 for i = 1:length(ITIlist)
 7     ITIcond = [ ITIcond repmat(ITIlist(i),1, ...
 8         (nTrials/nCond)/length(ITIlist)) ];
 9 end
10
11 for i = 1:nCond
12     ITIseq(i,:) = ITIcond(randperm(length(ITIcond)));
13 end
14 ITIseqCount = zeros(nCond,1);
15
16 seq = repmat(1:nCond,1,nTrials/nCond);
17
18 passed = 0;
19 nTry = 0;
20 while passed == 0
21     seq = seq(randperm(nTrials));
22     passed = 1;
23
24     i = 1;
25     while i < nTrials-2
26         if seq(i) == seq(i+1)
27             if seq(i+1) == seq(i+2)
28                 passed = 0;
29             end
30         end
31         i = i + 1;
32     end
```

(Continued)

(Continued)

```
33      nTry = nTry + 1;
34 end
35
36 for i = 1:length(seq)
37      ITIseqCount(seq(i)) = ITIseqCount(seq(i)) + 1;
38      iti(i) = ITIseq(seq(i),ITIseqCount(seq(i)));
39 end
40
41 seq
42 iti
42 nTry
44
45 % check
46 for i = 1:nCond
47      sort(iti(find(seq == i)))
48 end
```

Output:

```
 1 seq =
 2   Columns 1 through 10
 3      4      3      4      2      1      2      3      4      2      4
 4   Columns 11 through 20
 5      4      1      1      3      4      2      2      1      4      3
 6   Columns 21 through 30
 7      3      1      3      1      4      4      2      2      1      4
 8   Columns 31 through 40
 9      3      2      2      3      1      1      2      4      1      3
10   Columns 41 through 48
11      1      2      3      3      2      4      1      3
12 iti =
13   Columns 1 through 10
14      2      2      1      1      1      2      1      1      2      1
15   Columns 11 through 20
16      1      1      2      2      1      1      2      2      2      1
17   Columns 21 through 30
18      1      2      2      1      2      2      2      1      1      2
19   Columns 31 through 40
20      2      2      1      2      2      2      1      1      1      2
21   Columns 41 through 48
22      1      2      1      1      1      2      2      1
23 nTry =
24      7
25 ans =
26   Columns 1 through 10
```

```
27        1       1       1       1       1       1       2       2       2       2
28    Columns 11 through 12
29        2       2
30  ans =
31    Columns 1 through 10
32        1       1       1       1       1       1       2       2       2       2
33    Columns 11 through 12
34        2       2
35  ans =
36    Columns 1 through 10
37        1       1       1       1       1       1       2       2       2       2
38    Columns 11 through 12
39        2       2
40  ans =
41    Columns 1 through 10
42        1       1       1       1       1       1       2       2       2       2
43    Columns 11 through 12
44        2       2
```

Question 3

```
1  dlmwrite('trialinfo.txt',[ seq' iti' ],'\t')
2
3  figure
4
5  itiColor(1,:) = [ 0 0 0 ];
6  itiMark(1) = '^';
7  itiColor(2,:) = [ .25 .25 1 ];
8  itiMark(2) = 'o';
9
10 hold on
11 for i = 1:length(seq)
12     plot([i i],[0 max(seq)],'k');
13     plot([i i],[seq(i) seq(i)-1],'Color',itiColor(iti(i),:), ...
14     'LineWidth',3)
15     scatter(i,seq(i)-.5,150,itiMark(iti(i)),'k', ...
16         'MarkerFaceColor',itiColor(iti(i),:));
17 end
18
19 axis([0 length(seq)+1 0 max(seq)])
20 set(gca,'FontSize',24)
21 set(gca,'YTick',[1:max(seq)]-.5)
22 set(gca,'YTickLabel',1:max(seq))
```

(Continued)

(Continued)

```
23 set(gca,'XTick',0:6:length(seq))
24 set(gca,'TickDir','out')
25
26 xlabel('Trial Number')
27 ylabel('Condition')
28 box on
29
30 fp = fillPage(gcf, 'margins', [0 0 0 0], 'papersize', [25 4]);
31 print('trialSequence.pdf','-dpdf')
```

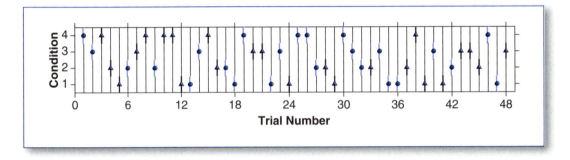

Question 4

Code:

```
1 nCond = 4;
2
3 seq
4 iti
5
6 trialInfo = seq + (iti-1)*nCond;
7 trialInfo
8
9 seq2 = mod(trialInfo-1,nCond) + 1
10 iti2 = ceil(trialInfo/nCond)
```

Output:

```
1 seq =
2   Columns 1 through 10
3      4     3     4     2     1     2     3     4     2     4
4   Columns 11 through 20
5      4     1     1     3     4     2     2     1     4     3
6   Columns 21 through 30
```

```
 7      3      1      3      1      4      4      2      2      1      4
 8    Columns 31 through 40
 9      3      2      2      3      1      1      2      4      1      3
10    Columns 41 through 48
11      1      2      3      3      2      4      1      3
12 iti =
13    Columns 1 through 10
14      2      2      1      1      1      2      1      1      2      1
15    Columns 11 through 20
16      1      1      2      2      1      1      2      2      2      1
17    Columns 21 through 30
18      1      2      2      1      2      2      2      1      1      2
19    Columns 31 through 40
20      2      2      1      2      2      2      1      1      1      2
21    Columns 41 through 48
22      1      2      1      1      1      2      2      1
23 trialInfo =
24    Columns 1 through 10
25      8      7      4      2      1      6      3      4      6      4
26    Columns 11 through 20
27      4      1      5      7      4      2      6      5      8      3
28    Columns 21 through 30
29      3      5      7      1      8      8      6      2      1      8
30    Columns 31 through 40
31      7      6      2      7      5      5      2      4      1      7
32    Columns 41 through 48
33      1      6      3      3      2      8      5      3
34 seq2 =
35    Columns 1 through 10
36      4      3      4      2      1      2      3      4      2      4
37    Columns 11 through 20
38      4      1      1      3      4      2      2      1      4      3
39    Columns 21 through 30
40      3      1      3      1      4      4      2      2      1      4
41    Columns 31 through 40
42      3      2      2      3      1      1      2      4      1      3
43    Columns 41 through 48
44      1      2      3      3      2      4      1      3
45 iti2 =
46    Columns 1 through 10
47      2      2      1      1      1      2      1      1      2      1
48    Columns 11 through 20
49      1      1      2      2      1      1      2      2      2      1
50    Columns 21 through 30
51      1      2      2      1      2      2      2      1      1      2
52    Columns 31 through 40
53      2      2      1      2      2      2      1      1      1      2
54    Columns 41 through 48
55      1      2      1      1      1      2      2      1
```

APPENDIX C

GLOSSARY

Through the course of this book, you've learned a lot about MATLAB. However, sometimes you need a bit of a refresher to remind you what a function does. Here I have included a glossary to give you a quick reminder of what each function discussed in the book does as well as refer you to the page where it was first encountered.

,

General operator. Separates inputs to a function (p. 27), values in a matrix (p. 5) or cell array (p. 41).

;

General operator. Separates rows when entering a matrix (p. 5) or used at the end of a command to suppress MATLAB from printing the output of the command to the Command Window (p. 8).

:

General operator. Tells MATLAB to use all values in the given dimension when calling a variable (p. 15) or when specifying a range of values (p. 8).

.*

Mathematical operator. Multiplies two variables together using element-wise multiplication (p. 11).

./

Mathematical operator. Divides one variable by another using element-wise division (p. 12).

'

Matrix operator. Transposes a matrix (p. 12).

( )

General operator. Used to specify the inputs to a function (p. 10) or the order of operations in a mathematical command (p. 10).

[ ]
General operator. Used to define a matrix (p. 5).

{ }
General operator. Used to define a cell array (p. 34).

%
General operator. Denotes the start of a single-line comment (p. 96).

%{
General operator. Starts a block comment (p. 96).

%}
General operator. Ends a block comment (p. 96).

=

General operator. Used to define variables (p. 5; also see p. 49).

==

Comparison/Boolean operator. Compares two numeric values and returns if they are equal (1) or not (0; p. 49).

<

Comparison/Boolean operator. Compares two numeric values and returns if the first is less than the second (1) or not (0; p. 49).

>

Comparison/Boolean operator. Compares two numeric values and returns if the first is greater than the second (1) or not (0; p. 49).

<=

Comparison/Boolean operator. Compares two numeric values and returns if the first is less than or equal to the second (1) or not (0; p. 49).

>=

Comparison/Boolean operator. Compares two numeric values and returns if the first is greater than or equal to the second (1) or not (0; p. 49).

~

General operator. Returns the opposite ("not") of a Boolean value (p. 49).

~=

Comparison/Boolean operator. Compares two numeric values and returns if they are not equal (1) or are equal (0; p. 52).

`ans`
General variable. Default variable where MATLAB returns values to, when no other is specified with the = operator (p. 4).

axis
Plotting function. Sets the axis boundaries (i.e., range of visible area) for the *x*- and *y*-dimensions of a figure (p. 71).

bar
Plotting function. Makes a bar graph from the specified data (p. 69).

barh
Plotting function. Makes a horizontal bar graph from the specified data (p. 73).

BarWidth
Plotting setting. Used with **set** or a plotting function to adjust the width of bars in a bar graph (p. 81).

box
Plotting function. Enables or disables the box around the figure (p. 87).

break
Debugging function. Breaks out of the current loop statement (p. 138).

cat
Matrix-manipulating function. Concatenates two matrices (p. 113).

cd
Directory function. Changes the present working directory to the specified directory (p. 24).

ceil
General function. Always rounds values up to the nearest integer (p. 10).

clc
General function. Clears the contents of the Command Window (p. 9).

clear
General function. Clears variables from the MATLAB workspace (p. 9).

close
Plotting function. Can close the current figure window, a specified figure window, or all figure windows (p. 84).

Color
Plotting setting. Used with **set** or a plotting function to adjust the color of line plots (pp. 79 and 87).

colorbar
Plotting function. Displays the mapping of colors to values used in an **image** plot (p. 78).

`colormap`

Plotting function. Used to modify the color shading in `image` plots (p. 82).

`contour`

Plotting function. Makes a contour plot from the specified data (p. 79).

`corr`

Inferential statistics function. Calculates Pearson's or Spearman's correlations on the specified data (p. 165).

`corrcoef`

Inferential statistics function. Calculates Pearson's correlations on the specified data (p. 165).

`dbquit`

Debugging function. Exits `keyboard` mode (p. 138).

`dir`

Directory function. Lists the contents of a directory (p. 22).

`disp`

Programming function. Prints the specified string to the MATLAB Command Window (p. 127).

`dlmread`

Data input/output function. Reads a text data file into MATLAB, using the specified delimiter (p. 26).

`dlmwrite`

Data input/output function. Writes a text data file out of MATLAB, using the specified delimiter (p. 41).

`doc`

Help function. Opens a separate, more detailed help window with an extensive description and more detailed examples than shown in `help` (p. 46).

`echo`

Debugging function. Echoes all commands run in a script or function to the Command Window. The same function is also used to disable `echo` (p. 93).

`EdgeColor`

Plotting setting. Used with `set` or a plotting function to adjust the edge color of bar graphs (p. 79).

`edit`

Programming function. Opens an editor window for modifying scripts and functions (p. 91).

else

Conditional statement. Executes a block of code only if previous conditions were not met (p. 96).

elseif

Conditional statement. Executes a block of code only if previous conditions are not met but that this specified condition is met (p. 96).

end

General function and conditional/looping statement. Can be used to refer to the last row or column when referring to values in a variable (p. 15) or to end a conditional statement (if—elseif—else) or loop (for/while; p. 97).

errorbar

Plotting function. Makes a line graph with error bars from the specified data (p. 75).

eval

Programming function. Evaluates a string as a MATLAB command; usually used in conjunction with sprintf (p. 120).

exit

General function. Exits MATLAB (p. 17).

FaceColor

Plotting setting. Used with set or a plotting function to adjust the color of bar graphs (p. 79).

fclose

Data input/output function. Closes a file that was opened with open (p. 30).

figure

Plotting function. Opens a new figure window or allows you to switch to an existing figure window (p. 84).

floor

General function. Always rounds values down to the nearest integer (p. 10).

FontSize

Plotting setting. Used with set or a plotting function to adjust the font size in figures (p. 86).

FontWeight

Plotting setting. Used with set or a plotting function to adjust the font weight (i.e., bold) in figures (p. 86).

`fopen`
Data input/output function. Opens a file to be read in with `textscan` or similar function (p. 30).

`for`
Looping statement. Loops through a block of code while a variable cycles through a specified set of values (p. 98).

`function`
Programming function. Defines a new function (p. 133).

`grid`
Plotting function. Enables or disables grid lines in the figure (p. 87).

`help`
Help function. Provides a description and examples for the specified function (p. 45).

`hold on`
Plotting function. Holds the current contents of the figure, rather than letting the figure get overwritten (p. 82).

`horzcat`
Matrix-manipulating function. Concatenates two matrices horizontally (p. 112).

`if`
Conditional statement. Executes a block of code only if a specified condition is met (p. 96).

`image`
Plotting function. Produces an image plot given a three-dimensional matrix, x- and y-axes, and color (p. 78).

`imagesc`
Plotting function. Produces an `image` plot, with the range of colors used automatically set to maximize differences (p. 78).

`input`
Programming function. Prompts the user to interactively input a variable, usually used within a script or function (p. 125).

`intersect`
Comparison function. Returns only the values that are in both of the specified variables (p. 54).

`isnan`
Comparison/Boolean function. Checks if values are NaNs; logically equivalent to `X == NaN` (though this would not work; p. 64).

keyboard
Programming function. Pauses a script or function and enters an interactive mode where the user can enter commands (p. 138).

legend
Plotting function. Adds a legend to the current figure, using the labels specified (p. 84).

length
General function. Determines the length of a matrix (i.e., largest number of rows or columns; is equivalent to `max(size(X))`; p. 47).

linespec
Plotting setting. Used with `help` to obtain a list of modifiable plotting settings (p. 82).

LineWidth
Plotting setting. Used with `set` or a plotting function to adjust the line width of lines in the figure (p. 81).

load
Data input/output function. Loads data from a text file or `.mat` file (p. 26).

lookfor
Help function. Searches for a specified string in MATLAB's help database (p. 45).

ls
Directory function. Lists the contents of a directory (p. 22).

MarkerEdgeColor
Plotting setting. Used with `set` or a plotting function to adjust the edge color of markers in a scatterplot (p. 82).

MarkerFaceColor
Plotting setting. Used with `set` or a plotting function to adjust the face color of markers in a scatterplot (p. 82).

MarkerSize
Plotting setting. Used with `set` or a plotting function to adjust the size of markers in a scatterplot (p. 82).

max
Descriptive statistics function. Returns the maximum value, across a given dimension, in a matrix (p. 47).

mean
Descriptive statistics function. Returns the mean/average value, across a given dimension, in a matrix (p. 45).

`median`
Descriptive statistics function. Returns the median value, across a given dimension, in a matrix (p. 47).

`min`
Descriptive statistics function. Returns the minimum value, across a given dimension, in a matrix (p. 47).

`mkdir`
Directory function. Makes a new directory using a specified string as the name, in the present working directory (p. 39).

`mod`
Mathematical operator. Calculates the modulo of one variable with another, that is, the division remainder (p. 148).

`nan`
Matrix-generating function. Creates a matrix of NaNs of the specified size (p. 103). NaN, in general, stands for "Not a Number" (p. 62).

`nanmean`
Descriptive statistics function. Same as `mean` but ignores NaNs (p. 65).

`nanmedian`
Descriptive statistics function. Same as `median` but ignores NaNs (p. 64).

`nanstd`
Descriptive statistics function. Same as `std` but ignores NaNs (p. 65).

`ones`
Matrix-generating function. Creates a matrix of ones of the specified size (p. 102).

`openvar`
General function. Allows you to interactively edit a variable using the GUI (p. 17).

`pause`
Programming function. Pauses MATLAB until a key is pressed for a specified amount of time in seconds (p. 138).

`pie`
Plotting function. Makes a pie graph from the specified data (p. 79).

`plot`
Plotting function. Makes a line graph from the specified data (p. 74).

`print`
Plotting function. Saves a figure to a file (p. 72).

profile
Debugging function. Creates a detailed report of which functions used how much processing time (p. 151).

pwd
Directory function. Returns the present working directory (i.e., path to the folder MATLAB is currently working in; p. 22).

quit
General function. Quits MATLAB (p. 17).

rand
Matrix-generating function. Creates a matrix of the specified size, consisting of random numbers drawn from a uniform distribution (p. 102).

randn
Matrix-generating function. Creates a matrix of the specified size, consisting of random numbers drawn from a normal distribution (p. 102).

repmat
Matrix-manipulating function. Returns a matrix that repeats an input matrix a specified number of times (p. 30).

reshape
Matrix-manipulating function. Returns a new matrix, based on a specified matrix, that is reorganized such that it contains the same total number of values with the values reshuffled across rows or columns (p. 171).

return
Programming function. Used within a function to specify a value that should be returned, before the function would otherwise be done running (p. 138).

round
General function. Rounds values up or down to the nearest integer, based on which integer is closer (p. 10).

save
Data input/output function. Saves variables from the MATLAB workspace to a specified .mat file (p. 40).

scatter
Plotting function. Makes a scatterplot from the specified data (p. 77).

set
Plotting function. Used to set a variety of plotting settings (p. 71).

setdiff
Comparison function. Returns only the values that are in the first variable but not the second (p. 54).

size
General function. Determines the size of a matrix (i.e., number of rows and columns; p. 47).

sort
Matrix-manipulating function. Sorts the values in a matrix (p. 47).

sprintf
Programming function. Constructs a string using values specified in other variables (p. 107).

squeeze
Matrix-manipulating function. Collapses a matrix across a dimension that only has a single index (p. 173).

std
Descriptive statistics function. Returns the standard deviation, across a given dimension (p. 47).

strcmp
Comparison/Boolean function. Compares two strings and returns if they are equal (1) or not (0; p. 57).

sum
Descriptive statistics function. Returns the sum, across a given dimension (p. 47).

textscan
Data input/output function. Reads in data from a loaded text file (p. 30).

tic
Debugging function. Starts a timer within MATLAB (p. 145).

TickDir
Plotting setting. Used with **set** or a plotting function to the axis-tick direction to go in or out of the figure (p. 86).

title
Plotting function. Sets the title for the current figure (p. 69).

toc
Debugging function. Stops a timer within MATLAB and returns the time elapsed (p. 145).

ttest
Inferential statistics function. Calculates a one-sample or paired-samples *t* test (p. 157).

ttest2
Inferential statistics function. Calculates an independent-samples *t* test (p. 163).

unique
Matrix-manipulating function. Returns the unique values from a variable, while also sorting them (p. 58).

var
Descriptive statistics function. Returns the variance, across a given dimension (p. 47).

vertcat
Matrix-manipulating function. Concatenates two matrices vertically (p. 112).

while
Looping statement. Loops through a block of code until a conditional statement is no longer satisfied (p. 101).

who
General function. Lists all of the variables in MATLAB's workspace (p. 9).

whos
General function. Lists all of the variables in MATLAB's workspace with more details than given by who (p. 104).

xlabel
Plotting function. Sets the *x*-axis label for the current figure (p. 69).

xlsread
Data input/output function. Reads in data from an Excel spreadsheet file (p. 39).

XTick
Plotting setting. Used with set or a plotting function to specify the *x*-tick positions (p. 71).

XTickLabel
Plotting setting. Used with set or a plotting function to specify the labels corresponding to *x*-tick positions (p. 71).

ylabel
Plotting function. Sets the *y*-axis label for the current figure (p. 69).

YTick

Plotting setting. Used with set or a plotting function to specify the y-tick positions (p. 71).

zeros

Matrix-generating function. Creates a matrix of zeros of the specified size (p. 102).

INDEX

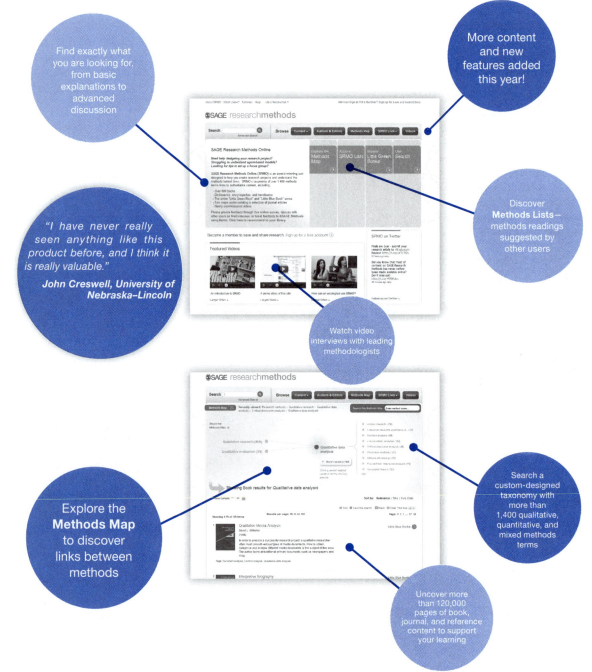

SAGE research**methods**

The essential online tool for researchers from the world's leading methods publisher

Find exactly what you are looking for, from basic explanations to advanced discussion

More content and new features added this year!

"I have never really seen anything like this product before, and I think it is really valuable."

John Creswell, University of Nebraska–Lincoln

Discover Methods Lists— methods readings suggested by other users

Watch video interviews with leading methodologists

Explore the Methods Map to discover links between methods

Search a custom-designed taxonomy with more than 1,400 qualitative, quantitative, and mixed methods terms

Uncover more than 120,000 pages of book, journal, and reference content to support your learning

Find out more at
www.sageresearchmethods.com